CITRUS

LOVERS

COOK BOOK

Compiled by
Bruce and Lee Fischer

**GOLDEN
WEST ✿
PUBLISHERS**

Acknowledgment

In preparing this book, we appreciate the cooperation and courtesies extended to us by **Lowell True**, Extension Agent, Agriculture, University of Arizona College of Agriculture, Maricopa County Office, Phoenix, Az.; **Terry H. Mikel**, Extension Agent, Agriculture, University of Arizona College of Agriculture, Yuma County Office, Yuma, Az.; **Glenda McGillis**, many of whose recipes have appeared earlier in her Citrus Cook Book; **Robert G. Platt**, Extension Subtropical Horticulturist, University of California, Dept. of Botany and Plant Sciences, Riverside, Calif.; **Jack Matthews**, State of Florida Dept. of Citrus, and **Francis J. Mulkeen**, Institutional and School Marketing Director, Dept. of Citrus, State of Florida, Lakeland, Fla.; **Richard R. Frisbie**, publisher of The Citrus Industry Magazine, Bartow, Fla.; **Gordon Smith**, Editor and Publisher, Citrus and Vegetable Magazine, Tampa, Fla.; **Paul M. Bailey**, Assistant Marketing Director, Texas Dept. of Agriculture, Austin, Tex.; **Gene Poll** and **Joanne Preziosi** of Dudley-Anderson-Yutzy Public Relations, Inc., New York, N.Y., and the myriad of friends whose recipes appear on these pages.

Printed in the United States of America

ISBN 0-914846-90-6

Golden West Publishers
4113 N. Longview Ave.
Phoenix, AZ 85014, USA
(602) 265-4392

CONTENTS

INTRODUCTION

Origin of the Orange

Oranges, as well as most species of citrus, had their native origin in China.

The fruit found its way by trade routes across the Gobi Desert, through India and ancient Persia, across North Africa and the Mediterranean isles into Italy, Spain and Portugal.

Columbus, on his second voyage to the New World, brought seeds of lemon, orange and citron to what is now Santo Domingo on the island of Haiti. From this point, oranges were dispersed among the Caribbean islands to Mexico and to Central and South America.

On the North American mainland, oranges appeared more than 400 years ago with the founding of St. Augustine, Florida, 1565, the oldest European community in the United States. Here, Spanish settlers planted the fruits of Spain: figs, olives, pomegranates, grapes and oranges. Oranges were planted in South Carolina (then called Santa Elena) in 1576.

During the sixteenth century, orange tree plantings were made in Vera Cruz, Mexico. From there, by way of Sonora and Baja, Mexico, the fruit traveled into Arizona and California.

Citrus growing in California began with the establishment of the first mission at San Diego in 1769. As the mission system grew, the Spanish friars brought oranges and other citrus fruits into other climatically favorable areas of the state. Orange groves were planted at the San Gabriel Mission near Los Angeles about 1804.

The first commercially profitable acreage was planted near Los Angeles in 1841. The population boom, stimulated by the Gold Rush of 1849, encouraged more plantings, but it was not until the 1880's that the industry matured in California. This was a result of the successful fruiting of the Washington navel orange at Riverside and completion of the first trans-continental rail service. The Washington navel became the all-time eating favorite. It is usually very large and easy to peel, has few (if any) seeds and is very sweet. These navels are identified by the "belly button" on the blossom end. It's a great eating orange and a favorite for salads. However, it is not a good cooking orange and does not freeze well. The juice is too heavy, and tends to separate.

Other navel varieties include the Australian, Double or Imperial, Egyptian, Melitensis, Parson, Summerfield and Surprise.

4

Meanwhile, the citrus industry in Florida was increasing in acreage, varieties and value. Commercial plantings became noteworthy about 1880. Both California and Florida were packing more than a million boxes a year by 1888. Texas reached a million boxes in 1929 and Arizona in 1934.

The American citrus belt now stretches across the warm, sunny areas of California, Arizona, Texas and Florida. In addition to this commercial growing belt, smaller plantings and citrus in home gardens are found in southern Nevada, southern Utah, New Mexico, near the Gulf Coast of Louisiana, Mississippi and Alabama, and along the coast and on the islands off the coast of Georgia and South Carolina.

Sweet Oranges

Valencias are the favorite juice orange, and the nation's largest sweet orange crop. They have few seeds and the juice is sweet and tangy. Valencia juice consistency is great for freezing.

Other sweet orange varieties, sometimes called "Mediterranean oranges," include the Bessie, Centennial, Circassian, Du Roi, Everbearing, Exquisite, Hamlin, Jaffa, Joppa, Lue Gim Gong, Majorca, Maltese Oval, Marquis, Paper Rind, Pineapple, Prata, Star Calyx, and many, many more.

Sour Oranges

The Sour Orange, also known as the Seville or Spanish Orange, grows abundantly on large, hardy trees in Spain, Cuba, Puerto Rico and in many areas of the North American Sun Belt.

Trees are often planted to enhance greenery and may be used as hedges. Since they are so hardy, they are often used as root stock for grafting other varieties of citrus. In fact, a "cocktail tree" is often created by grafting several kinds of oranges, tangerines, grapefruit and lemons to a sour orange tree.

Varieties of Spanish oranges include: Acme, Arcadia, Boone, Dummitt, Early Oblong, Enterprise, Foster, Hick, Homosassa, Indian River, Madame Vinous, Magnum Bonum, May, Nonpareil, Old Vini, Osceola, Parson Brown and Stark. Some of these, by hybridization, have become a sweeter and more desirable fruit.

Blood Oranges

Blood Oranges are grown mainly as a novelty, although they have a tangy, sweet flavor. They are small to medium size with pale skin. The juice and pulp are a rich, ruby-red color.

They are closely related to the Mediterranean oranges and include such varieties as Maltese, Ruby, Sanford Blood, Saul Blood and St. Michael.

Tangerines

A tangerine by any other name is a Mandarin orange. Both names are used interchangeably for the "zipper-skin orange."

Chinese Mandarin oranges were brought to Louisiana by the Italian consul at New Orleans in the 1840's. From there, the orange was introduced into Florida about 1854.

Popularity of the fruit is due to the fact that it is so easy to eat. The peel slips off of the fruit easily, segments pull apart easily and it can be eaten just like candy. Of course, the tangerine is far more wholesome than other sweets, and the fruit of the tangerine is sweet and refreshing.

Varieties include the Dancy tangerine, Satsuma orange, China, Beauty, Cleopatra, Oneco, and hybrid varieties like the King, Tangerona and the Temple orange.

The Kinnow tangerine is a newcomer to the field, having been developed in California in 1935 and perfected in Yuma, Arizona. Smooth and thin-skinned, the flesh is full, close-packed, juicy and very sweet in late season.

Tangelos

A cross between grapefruit and Dancy Tangerine, the tangelo was first developed in 1901, and perfected with other hybrid varieties during the 1908-1912 period.

Varieties include the Minneola, Nocatee, Orlando, Sampson, Seminole and Thornton.

Genesis of the Grapefruit

The native home of the grapefruit is quite obscure. One story is that a certain Capt. Shaddock was returning to England from a voyage to India. On board he carried seeds of a large citrus fruit he found somewhere in the Orient or Polynesia. These seeds were planted on the island of Barbados. The fruit that the resulting trees bore were subsequently called "Shaddock." From there, the fruit found its way to Florida in the early nineteenth century, but was considered of little commercial value at the time.

Somewhere along the line, a mutant occurred that we now call the "grapefruit," a superior fruit. Plantings increased and production reached a million boxes soon after the Civil War. By 1893, more than five million boxes were shipped to New York, Philadelphia and other northern cities, and Florida had a new and thriving industry.

The Marsh grapefruit, developed in Florida during the 1890's, has since become the major grapefruit, not only in Florida, but also as the desert grapefruit of California and Arizona. Its popularity is due to its few seeds, good

6

fruit shape and high quality. Most growers are now harvesting fruit from the Marsh Seedless or the Pink Seedless.

Texas has built its grapefruit industry on production of pink and red varieties. Grown in the heart of the lower Rio Grande valley, the Ruby Red variety constitutes 95 percent of the grapefruit grown in Texas groves. In 1929, the Ruby Red fruit was discovered growing on a pink grapefruit tree.

Other varieties of grapefruit include the Duncan, Redblush, DeSoto, Aurantium, Excelsior, Foster, Hall, Josselyn, Leonardy, Manville, May, McCarty, McKinley, Pernambuco, Royal, Triumph, Walters and others.

Lifeline of the Lemon

Traveling from the Orient to Sicily, Corsica, Genoa and other parts of southern Europe, and introduced into America by Spaniards, the lemon has become so prolific in its New World surroundings that it now grows wild in southern Florida and the West Indies.

The lemon was doing quite well in Florida until the big freeze in 1894-95 wiped out much of Florida's plantings that have since been replaced by other citrus crops. California and Arizona growers now produce about 62% of the nation's lemons. Actually, lemons make up half of all citrus grown in the Yuma area of Arizona, while the Eureka lemon is most commanly planted in coastal areas of California.

Other varieties of lemons include Lisbon, Villafranca, Meyer, Everbearing, Genoa, Otaheite, Ponderosa, Rough, Sicily, Sweet, Prior, Frost Nucellar, Rosenberger, Monroe and Limonera.

Time for Lime

Often confused with the lemon, the lime is actually a distinct fruit. It was introduced into the West Indies by Spain. There the tree succeeds on poor, sandy soils but is easily injured by cold.

Used in limeade and for seasoning foods, the fruit is usually some shade of green, even when ripe, although Florida does grow a yellow lime and Arizona grows the rangphur lime which looks like a very small orange.

Varieties also include the Bearrs, Mexican, Tahiti, Kusaie, Eustis Limequat and Calamondin.

The Calamondin is a small tree or shrub fruit often used in place of lemon or lime. It was introduced into the Untied States from the Philippines. The fruit is small with a thin peel, attractive but highly acid. The limequat is a cross of the lime with a kumquat.

Citron—the Oldtimer

Mercenaries of ancient Greece first discovered the citron growing in Persia. Its seed was spread from there to Palestine, Greece, Italy and the Mediterranean islands.

It is most notable for its chewy candied peel used in fruit cake and confections. Formerly cultivated in Florida and California, it is now grown commercially only in California.

Varieties include Corsican, Etrog, Lemon, Lyman and Orange.

What is a Quat?

Kumquats are small citrus fruits, oblong in shape, one to three inches long. They originated in Japan and were introduced into Europe in 1846 and into Florida in 1885.

They are borne on hardy, small trees. The fruit contains large amounts of pectin, making it easy to preserve. Kumquats may be eaten raw, whole, including pulp and the thin rind. Just like eating a grape! The trees are often grown in pots and tubs.

Kumquat varieties include Nagami, Maruni, Hong Kong and Meiwa.

How to Peel
and Section Citrus

Using a sharp knife, cut off both ends of the citrus fruit. Set fruit on flat end and strip away peel by cutting from top to bottom along the curvature of the fruit. Cut deep enough to remove the white membranes. Loosen the segments by cutting gently along each section to the center of the fruit. Lift each section out from the center.

Drying Citrus Peel

Reserve some of the peel after juicing the fruit. Grate peel or put through a food chopper set for coarse grind. Spread grated peel on paper towel and let dry overnight. Place peel in cheesecloth or mesh square and tie corners. Hang until dry. Dried peel can be stored in a covered container or left to hang in its drying bag.

This dried peel can be used for seasoning when cooking. If fresh grated peel is called for and it is out of season for fresh fruit, put a small amount of dried peel in a small cup, add a little water and let peel sit until plump. Use as recipe directs.

Grapefruit Shrimp Cocktail

Halve grapefruit. Remove core. Loosen the sections, without cutting the membrane from the skin, and remove every other section. Fill empty sections with cooked shrimp and thin slice of peeled avocado. Fill center of grapefruit with Russian Dressing and garnish with parsley.

Lemony Cocktail

½ cup SUGAR
1 cup WATER
¼ cup RED JELLY
¼ cup LEMON JUICE
3 cups FRUIT (diced)

Boil sugar, water and red jelly for five minutes and chill. Add lemon juice and pour mixture over diced fruits.

Grilled Grapefruit

Cut grapefruit in halves crosswise. Cut around each section with a sharp knife. Snip out center with shears.

#1

Sprinkle each half with one tablespoon sugar and a dash of cinnamon. Dot with one tablespoon butter.

#2

Spread each half with one tablespoons mashed mint, currant or apple jelly.

#3

Spread each half with one tablespoon honey or molasses.

Place grapefruit on broiler rack 3 to 4 inches from flame. Broil 10 to 15 minutes (or until grapefruit is slightly brown and heated through). Grapefruit may also be baked in a 400 F oven for 15 minutes.

Crab-Grapefruit Cocktail

Salad GREENS
2 cans (7¾ oz. each) CRAB MEAT
3 cups GRAPEFRUIT SECTIONS
RUSSIAN DRESSING

Line six cocktail glasses with salad greens. Divide crab meat (drained) and grapefruit sections among the glasses. Serve with dressing. (6 servings)

Tangy Seafood Cocktail

1 cup SHRIMP (cleaned/cooked)
½ cup CELERY (cut fine)
¾ cup KETCHUP
1 teaspoon WORCESTERSHIRE
   SAUCE
¼ cup LEMON JUICE
1 tablespoon ONION (minced)

Combine all ingredients and mix thoroughly. Chill and serve in cocktail glasses with lemon quarters. (Serves 4)

Grapefruit Antipasto

6 GRAPEFRUIT
2 AVOCADOS
1 lb. SHRIMP
2 CUCUMBERS
1 pint CHERRY TOMATOES
1 bunch SCALLIONS
1 pint COTTAGE CHEESE

Use a three or four-tier serving platter. Arrange all ingredients separately on platter. Serve with dressing. Sprinkle juice from sectioned grapefruit over avocado to prevent discoloration. (To prepare fruit: section grapefruit and chill. Peel and slice avocados. Cook, clean and chill shrimp. Score and slice cucumbers. Trim scallions.)

Citrus Fruit Cocktail

3 ORANGES
1 GRAPEFRUIT
2 tablespoons POWDERED SUGAR

Segment oranges and grapefruit and mix well with sugar.
Refrigerate and serve ice cold in cocktail glasses. (Serves 4)

Orange Fruit Soup

2 tablespoons TAPIOCA (quick-cook)
2½ cups ORANGE JUICE
2 tablespoons SUGAR
Dash of SALT
2 CINNAMON STICKS
1½ cups ORANGE SECTIONS (with
    juice)
1 pkg. (12 oz.) Frozen Sliced
    PEACHES
1 BANANA (sliced)

Combine tapioca, orange juice, sugar and salt in saucepan. Let
stand 5 minutes. Add cinnamon sticks. Bring to a boil over
medium heat. Remove from heat; cool 20 minutes. Remove
cinnamon sticks and add peaches (thawed, cut in pieces) and
banana. Heat and serve. (6 to 8 servings)

Citrus Fruit Soup

1 can (1 lb. 14 oz.) RED
    PLUMS
1 can (1 lb. 14 oz.) FRUIT
    COCKTAIL
1 can (13½ oz.) PINEAPPLE
    BITS
1 can (16 oz.) RED SOUR
    CHERRIES
¾ cup RAISINS
2 cups PINEAPPLE JUICE
1 cup ORANGE JUICE
1 ORANGE (thinly sliced)
1 LEMON (thinly sliced)
1 pkg. (3 oz.) CHERRY
    GELATIN
3 tablespoons TAPIOCA
    (quick-cook)

In a saucepan, combine the undrained canned fruits and
remaining ingredients. Mix well and heat to a boiling point.
Simmer 15 minutes more and serve either warm or cold. (Serves
12)

Chicken Rice Lemon Soup

**4 cans condensed CHICKEN BROTH
(undiluted)
¼ cup raw RICE
2 EGGS (beaten)
3 tablespoons fresh LEMON JUICE
½ teaspoon fresh LEMON PEEL
(grated)
1 fresh LEMON (sliced very thin)**

Combine chicken broth and rice. Cover and simmer until rice is tender. Meanwhile, beat eggs and lemon juice. Pour two cups of hot broth very slowly into egg-lemon mixture. Return egg mixture to saucepan with rice, and add lemon peel. Reheat, but do not boil. Serve immediately in soup bowls and float lemon slice in each bowl.

Preparing Citrus for Garnish

Here are some basic tips for serving fresh citrus:

How to Section Oranges

Cut slices from top, then cut off peel in strips from top to bottom, cutting deeply enough to remove white membrane. Then cut slice from bottom. Or cut off peel round and round, spiral fashion. Go over fruit again, removing any remaining white membrane. Cut along side of each dividing membrane from outside to middle of core. Remove section by section over bowl to retain juice.

Preparing Orange Wedges

Wash orange; do not peel. Cut into 6 or 8 wedges, depending on size of orange. For snacking, serve plain or dipped in honey or cinnamon-sugar mixture. To make orange "smiles," peel back ends of each wedge about 1-inch.

Preparing Grapefruit Halves

Cut fruit in half; remove core if desired. Cut around each section, loosening fruit from membrane. Do not cut around entire outer edge of fruit.

SALADS & DRESSINGS

Sunshine Salad

6 cups torn SALAD GREENS
2 cups GRAPEFRUIT (sectioned)
6 slices BACON (cooked, crumbled)
SALAD DRESSING

Place salad greens in large bowl. Place grapefruit sections on top of greens and sprinkle bacon over sections. Serve with dressing. (6 servings)

Salad for Slimmers

4 cups COTTAGE CHEESE
   (uncreamed)
2 tablespoons CELERY (minced)
1 tablespoon CHIVES (minced)
1 tablespoon RED PEPPER (chopped)
½ teaspoon SALT
¼ teaspoon PEPPER
4 cups ORANGE SECTIONS (drained)

Toss all ingredients together EXCEPT orange sections. Refrigerate one hour to allow flavors to blend. Place salad in large serving bowl and garnish with orange sections. Serve with Low-Calorie Dressing. (Serves 4)

Low-Calorie Citrus Dressing

2 teaspoons CORNSTARCH
1 teaspoon SUGAR
¾ teaspoon SALT
½ teaspoon PAPRIKA
½ teaspoon DRY MUSTARD
1 cup ORANGE JUICE
2 tablespoons SALAD OIL
¼ teaspoon TABASCO
¼ cup KETCHUP

Combine dry ingredients in saucepan. Stir in orange juice. Place over medium heat and bring to a boil, stirring constantly. Boil one minute and remove from heat. Stir in remaining ingredients and chill before serving. (Makes 1¼ cups)

13

Grapefruit Turkey Salad

2 GRAPEFRUIT
2 tablespoons GRAPEFRUIT JUICE
3 cups TURKEY (cooked, diced)
1 cup CELERY (diced)
1 cup Seedless GRAPES
½ teaspoon SALT
½ teaspoon CURRY
½ cup MAYONNAISE

Peel and section grapefruits. Reserve juice. Combine turkey, grapes and salt. Add grapefruit sections and juice. Cover and refrigerate one hour.

Combine curry powder and mayonnaise. Blend thoroughly. Add to turkey mixture and toss to coat evenly. Serve in lettuce cups. (Serves 4)

Salmon Surprise

1 envelope plain GELATIN
1 cup ORANGE JUICE
1 EGG (well beaten)
1 small can SALMON (flaked)
2 cups GRAPEFRUIT SEGMENTS

Dissolve gelatin in orange juice. Heat in top of double boiler until well dissolved. Slowly add beaten egg and salt. Cook in double boiler until slightly thickened, stirring constantly. Set aside to cool. When cooled, add salmon. Fold in grapefruit segments, broken up and drained. Pour into slightly greased glass loaf pan. Put in refrigerator to congeal. Serve on bed of shredded lettuce.

Turkey Salad

½ cup MAYONNAISE
ORANGE JUICE
2 cups TURKEY (cooked, cubed)
1 cup CELERY (sliced)
1 cup fresh ORANGE SLICES

Mix mayonnaise with orange juice to desired thinness. Combine mayonnaise with other ingredients, toss, and chill. Serve on lettuce, garnished with orange segments. (Tuna or chicken can be used in place of turkey.)

Grapefruit Artichoke Salad

1 GRAPEFRUIT
¼ teaspoon ONION (grated)
1 can (8-oz.) ARTICHOKE HEARTS
3 tablespoons FRENCH DRESSING

Prepare grapefruit and break into sections. Chill. Add grated onion to French dressing. Marinate artichoke hearts in dressing about one hour. Arrange with grapefruit sections on lettuce and serve.

Citrus Onion Salad

4 ORANGES
2 GRAPEFRUIT
2 ONIONS
4 cups SPINACH LEAVES (torn)
2 cups SALAD GREENS (torn)

Chill fruit before preparing. Section fruit, drain thoroughly. Slice onions and separate slices into rings. Arrange citrus sections and onion rings on mixed greens. Serve with dressing. (Serves 6)

Orange-Cranberry Mold

1 pkg. (3 oz.) Orange-Flavor GELATIN
1 cup BOILING WATER
½ cup ORANGE JUICE
1 ORANGE
1 can (16 oz.) CRANBERRY SAUCE
 (whole)
½ cup CELERY (chopped)

Dissolve gelatin in boiling water and add orange juice. Chill until the consistency of unbeaten egg white. Cut orange in quarters, remove seeds and put through food chopper. Combine ground orange, cranberry sauce and celery in gelatin mixture. Turn into one-quart mold. Chill until firm. Umold to serve. (About 8 servings)

15

Orange Toss

7 cups SALAD GREENS
2 cups ORANGE SECTIONS (fresh)
½ ONION (sliced)

Combine salad greens (romaine, Boston lettuce, red leaf lettuce) with orange sections and onion rings. Serve wtih dressing. (Makes 6 servings)

Orange and Carrot Salad

2 tablespoons unflavored GELATIN
½ cup COLD WATER
2 cups BOILING WATER
½ teaspoon SALT
1 tablespoon SUGAR
1 tablespoon LEMON JUICE
2 tablespoons VINEGAR
1 cup ORANGE JUICE (and pulp)
1 cup CARROTS (grated)

Soak the gelatin in cold water for five minutes. Add all ingredients EXCEPT CARROTS, and chill. When partly jelled, stir in the carrots, and pour into serving mold. Refrigerate to set. To serve, turn out from mold and serve on lettuce leaves with favorite dressing.

Jellied Vegetable Salad

2 tablespoons unflavored GELATIN
6 tablespoons COLD WATER
1½ cups BOILING WATER
1 cup ORANGE JUICE
6 tablespoons LEMON JUICE
¼ cup SUGAR
½ teaspoon SALT
1 cup PEAS (cooked)
1 cup CARROTS (cooked, diced)

Soak gelatin in cold water five minutes. Add boiling water, orange and lemon juices, sugar and salt. Cool. When slightly thickened, add vegetables and pour into individual molds. Chill until firm and serve with dressing. (Serves 8)

Tangerine Cole Slaw

2 cups TANGERINES (sectioned)
3 cups CABBAGE (shredded)
½ cup RAISINS
1/3 cup MAYONNAISE
½ teaspoon SALT
2 teaspoons SUGAR
½ teaspoon CELERY SEED

Chill tangerines before preparing. Peel and remove white membrane. Pull sections apart. Cut off center section membrane with scissors. Cut sections in half and add to cabbage and raisins. Combine remaining ingredients and add to cabbage, mixing well. Chill and serve. (Serves 6)

Lemony Cole Slaw

2½ cups CABBAGE (chopped)
¾ teaspoon SALT
Dash of PEPPER
1½ tablespoons SUGAR
6 tablespoons LIGHT CREAM
3 tablespoons LEMON JUICE

Combine all ingredients and chill thoroughly before serving. (Makes 6 servings)

Orange Waldorf Salad

1 quart APPLES (diced)
2 tablespoons LEMON JUICE
1 cup CELERY (diced)
2 cups ORANGES (peeled, diced)
½ cup RAISINS
½ cup NUTMEATS
1 cup MAYONNAISE

Marinate apples in lemon juice. Combine apples with remainder of ingredients and serve on lettuce cups. (Serves 12)

Grapefruit-Tuna Salad

2 cans (7-oz.) TUNA (in water)
1 CUCUMBER (sliced)
3 cups GRAPEFRUIT (sectioned)
1 cup Cherry TOMATOES

Mound chunks of drained tuna in middle of platter. Arrange cucumber slices around edge of platter. Fill in area around tuna with grapefruit sections and tomatoes. Serve with Garden Dressing.

Garden Dressing

3 tablespoons ONION (chopped fine)
1 tablespoon GREEN PEPPER (chopped)
1 tablespoon PARSLEY (chopped)

6 tablespoons Frozen GRAPEFRUIT JUICE concentrate (thawed, undiluted)
¼ cup WATER
2 tablespoons SALAD OIL
¼ teaspoon SALT

Mix all ingredients together in bowl or covered jar. Allow flavors to blend at least one hour before serving. (Makes 3/4 cup)

Basic French Dressing

½ teaspoon SALT
¼ teaspoon PAPRIKA
4 tablespoons OIL
2 tablespoons LEMON JUICE

Combine ingredients in order given and shake thoroughly in screw-top jar.

Russian Dressing

3 tablespoons MAYONNAISE
2 tablespoons OLIVE OIL
1 tablespoon LEMON JUICE
1 tablespoon KETCHUP
2 drops TABASCO SAUCE

Combine mayonnaise with other ingredients, stirring constantly until smooth.

Cooked Citrus Dressing

3 tablespoons FLOUR
2 tablespoons SUGAR
¾ teaspoon DRY MUSTARD
½ teaspoon SALT
1 cup ORANGE JUICE
2 EGG YOLKS (well beaten)
1 tablespoon BUTTER
¼ cup LEMON JUICE

Mix flour, sugar, mustard, salt, orange juice and egg yolks thoroughly and cook in top of double boiler until thickened. Add butter and lemon juice. Stir, remove from heat and refrigerate. Use as dressing for fruit salads. (Makes 1½ cups)

Orange-Honey French Dressing

¼ cup ORANGE JUICE Frozen
   Concentrate
1 tablespoon VINEGAR
¼ cup HONEY
½ teaspoon DRY MUSTARD
½ teaspoon SALT
2/3 cup SALAD OIL

Mix all ingredients thoroughly, EXCEPT salad oil. Add the oil slowly, while beating constantly with rotary or electric beater. Refrigerate until used. (Makes about 1¼ cups)

Thousand Island Dressing

½ cup OLIVE OIL
JUICE ½ LEMON
JUICE ½ ORANGE
1 teaspoon ONION (grated)
1 tablespoon PARSLEY
  (chopped)
8 sliced OLIVES
8 cooked CHESTNUTS
¼ teaspoon SALT
¼ teaspoon PAPRIKA
1 teaspoon
  WORCESTERSHIRE
  SAUCE
¼ teaspoon MUSTARD

Remove shells from chestnuts, and cook in boiling salted water until soft; then cool, and cut in thin slices. Put all the ingredients in a pint glass jar; cover, and shake until smooth and slightly thickened.

Sunfruit Cup

6 fresh ORANGES (unpeeled)
2 cups Thompson seedless GRAPES
½ cup grated COCONUT
½ cup WHIPPING CREAM
3 tablespoons SUGAR
2 tablespoons fresh LEMON JUICE
2 tablespoons fresh grated
    ORANGE RIND

Cut 1/2 inch slice from top of each orange. Remove pulp from oranges and scrape white membrane out with a spoon. Remove seeds and membranes from orange pulp. Add grated orange rind to chilled whipping cream and whip until it forms soft mounds. Add lemon juice and sugar. Fold in orange pulp, grapes and coconut. Spoon into orange shells. Garnish with maraschino cherry.

Lemon Salad Dressing

1 clove GARLIC (minced)
2 teaspoons SALT
1 teaspoon BLACK PEPPER
¼ teaspoon SUGAR
½ teaspoon fresh LEMON PEEL
    (grated)
½ cup fresh LEMON JUICE
1¼ cups SALAD OIL

Combine all ingredients in jar and shake. Store in covered container in refrigerator until needed. (Will keep from four to five weeks.)

Guacamole Dip

2 large, ripe AVOCADOS
3 tablespoons LIME JUICE
1 teaspoon SALT
¼ cup ONION (minced)
1 can (4 oz.) GREEN CHILES
    (chopped)
1 small TOMATO (diced)

Place all ingredients in blender. Blend until mixture is thick and creamy. Serve with corn chips or potato chips.

Heavenly Frost Salad

1 can (1 lb. 13 oz.) cling
   PEACH HALVES
1 cup halved, seeded Tokay GRAPES
1 tablespoon ORANGE PEEL (grated)
3 ORANGES (sectioned)
¾ cup LEMON JUICE
¾ cup HONEY
LETTUCE (or watercress)

Drain peaches and place in large refrigerator tray or shallow pan. Add halved grapes. Sprinkle with orange peel. Add sectioned orange slices. Combine lemon juice and honey and pour over all. Set in freezing compartment until fruit is almost icy and the syrup mushy (about one hour).

Arrange lettuce or watercress on serving platter or on individual serving plates. Place fruit on lettuce bed and top with frosty syrup.

Pima Wilted Salad

4 slices BACON
3 medium ORANGES
   (cut into pieces)
3 tablespoons fresh
   LEMON JUICE
1 tablespoon SUGAR
1 teaspoon SALT
¼ ONION (chopped)
½ cup SWISS CHEESE
   (cut into thin strips)
1 head LETTUCE

Fry bacon until crisp. Remove from pan, drain, and crumble. Add lemon juice, sugar, salt and onion to hot bacon drippings. Heat until onion is transparent but not brown. Tear lettuce into bite-size pieces into a large bowl. Pour the hot mixture over the lettuce. Add fried bacon, orange pieces, and Swiss cheese. Toss lightly. Serve at once.

Royal Fruit Salad

2 cups fresh ORANGES
   (peeled and diced)
1 cup
   PINEAPPLE CHUNKS
1 cup Thompson seedless
   GRAPES
1 cup miniature
   MARSHMALLOWS
1/3 cup COCONUT (flaked)
2 cups SOUR CREAM
¼ teaspoon SALT
LETTUCE

Combine all ingredients. Stir in sour cream and salt. Chill overnight. Just before serving, stir lightly and spoon onto lettuce bed.

21

Citrus Fruit Dressing

3 tablespoons LEMON JUICE
3 tablespoons ORANGE JUICE
3 to 4 tablespoons SALAD OIL
¼ teaspoon SALT
1 tablespoon SUGAR

Combine all ingredients and mix thoroughly. Pour over fruit salad. (Makes 1/2 cup)

Lemon Mayonnaise

1 EGG
¼ cup LEMON JUICE
1 teaspoon MUSTARD
1 teaspoon SALT
1 teaspoon SUGAR
Dash of PEPPER
1 pint of SALAD OIL

Combine egg, lemon juice, mustard, salt, sugar, and pepper. Slowly beat in salad oil, using hand beater. Beat until dressing is thickened. (Makes 2 cups)

Orange-Cranberry Relish

1 can (6 oz.) Frozen concentrated
   ORANGE JUICE (thawed)
1 lb. FROZEN CRANBERRIES
2 cups SUGAR
1 cup WATER

Combine all ingredients in a saucepan and bring to a boil. Lower heat and simmer until berries are tender (about 15 minutes). Cool, cover and refrigerate. (About 4 cups)

SEAFOOD

Orange-Poached Trout

2 cups ORANGE JUICE
2 cups WATER
3 tablespoons WINE
VINEGAR
1 ONION (sliced)
1½ teaspoons SALT
(divided)
6 PEPPERCORNS
(whole)
2 ALLSPICE (whole)
1 BAY LEAF

3 sprigs PARSLEY
2 Large TROUT
2 tablespoons BUTTER
3 tablespoons ONION
(chopped)
2 tablespoons PARSLEY
(chopped)
¼ teaspoon
TARRAGON
2 tablespoons FLOUR

In large skillet, bring orange juice, water, vinegar, onion and one teaspoon salt to a boil. Tie peppercorns, allspice, bay leaf and parsley in cheesecloth. Add to skillet and simmer 30 minutes. Add trout and simmer (covered) from 6 to 8 minutes (or til fish flakes). Remove trout to serving platter and keep warm. Remove cheesecloth bag from liquid.

In small saucepan melt butter, onion, parsley, tarragon and remaining salt. Cook, stirring constantly, until onion is tender. Blend in flour and cook two minutes. Gradually stir in poaching liquid and cook until mixture thickens and comes to a boil. Pour over trout and serve. (4 servings)

Broiled Pan-Dressed Fish

3 lbs. FISH (fresh or frozen)
¼ cup OIL
¼ cup LEMON JUICE
1½ teaspoons SALT
¾ teaspoon PAPRIKA

Clean, wash and dry fresh fish, or thaw frozen fish.

Combine oil and seasonings. Place fish on well-greased broiler pan. Brush fish inside and out with seasoned oil. Broil about four inches from heat, from five to eight minutes. Turn fish carefully and brush on remaining oil. Broil five to eight minutes longer (or until fish flakes easily). (Serves 6)

Shrimp Curry

1 pkg. (12-oz.) frozen SHRIMP
1 tablespoon BUTTER
1½ teaspoons CURRY POWDER
1¼ teaspoons SALT
1 medium TOMATO (chopped)
1 medium ONION (chopped)
2 tablespons LIME JUICE
1 cup SOUR CREAM
3 AVOCADOS

Cook shrimp as package directs. In a saucepan, melt butter with curry powder and salt. Add tomato and onions and cook until soft. Add lime juice, shrimp and sour cream. Heat thoroughly and serve on halved avocados. (Serves 6)

Shrimp
with Orange Tarragon Sauce

3 pounds large SHRIMP
1 cup MAYONNAISE
1 cup SOUR CREAM
¼ cup frozen ORANGE JUICE
    concentrate (thawed, undiluted)
2 tablespoons ONION (chopped)
1 teaspoon dried leaf TARRAGON

Clean, cook and chill shrimp. Blend mayonnaise with sour cream and orange juice. Stir in onion and tarragon. Chill. Serve with shrimp. (Serves 8)

Baked Fish Fillets

2 lbs. FISH FILLETS (fresh or frozen)
2 tablespoons OIL
2 tablespoons LEMON JUICE
1 teaspoon SALT
½ teaspoon PAPRIKA

Thaw frozen fish and separate into six portions. Place fish in a single layer, skin side down, in a well-greased baking dish. Combine remaining ingredients and pour over fish. Bake at 350 F from 20 to 25 minutes (or until fish flakes easily). (Serves 6)

Fish in Lemon Aspic

2 tablespoons unflavored GELATIN
¼ cup COLD WATER
1½ cups BOILING WATER
½ teaspoon SALT
1 tablespoon SUGAR
½ cup LEMON JUICE
1 cup FISH (cooked, flaked)
1 cup CELERY (chopped)

Sprinkle gelatin in cold water. Add boiling water, salt, sugar and lemon juice. Cool thoroughly and add fish and celery. Pour into individual molds and serve (unmolded) on lettuce cups. (Makes 4 servings)

Lemon Rice Fishbake

1½ cups precooked RICE
1 ONION (chopped)
1 cup CELERY (sliced)
1/3 cup BUTTER
¼ teaspoon THYME
1½ teaspoons SALT
⅛ teaspoon PEPPER
2 teaspoons fresh
　LEMON PEEL (grated)
¼ cup fresh LEMON JUICE
1 (3 to 6 lb.) whole FISH
　(cleaned)

Boil rice until tender. Drain. While rice is cooking, saute onion and celery in butter until onion is golden brown. Add thyme, salt, pepper, lemon peel and juice. Mix well and steam with small amount of water (about five minutes). Add rice and mix. Stuff cleaned fish with rice. Place in covered baking pan and bake in 325 F oven until fish is done.

For an unusual taste, try using grapefruit slices against the sides of fish. Or, try grapefruit juice, in place of the usual lemon.

Lime Butter

½ cup BUTTER (softened)
2 tablespoons PARSLEY (chopped)
4 tablespoons fresh LIME JUICE
Dash of CAYENNE

Cream butter and add remaining ingredients. (Store in refrigerator until needed.) Serve with fish, steaks or vegetables such as cabbage, carrots, green beans and over green lima beans. Use your imagination, and you will never want to be without a fresh lime in your kitchen.

25

Lemon Clam Fritters

¼ cup FLOUR
½ teaspoon BAKING POWDER
1 EGG
6 tablespoons fresh LEMON JUICE
1½ cups minced CLAMS
   (canned - do not drain)
SALAD OIL

Blend flour, baking powder, egg, lemon juice, clams and clam juice. Heat enough oil in large frypan to cover 1/4 inch deep, until hot. Drop batter by teaspoon into hot oil and cook until browned on both sides. Lift from oil and drain on paper towels. Keep warm until all the batter is cooked. (Add more oil to pan during cooking, if necessary.)

Baked Fish with Lime

2 lbs. WHITE FISH FILLETS
   (halibut, turbot, etc.)
1½ teaspoons SALT
¼ teaspoon PEPPER
8 tablespoons OLIVE OIL
1/3 cup fresh LIME JUICE
Chopped GREEN ONIONS
Chopped PARSLEY

Sprinkle fish fillets with salt and pepper. Place fish in shallow baking pan which has been lightly greased. Combine olive oil and lime juice. Brush on fish to coat entirely. Sprinkle chopped green onions over top.

Place in 350 F oven and bake uncovered until fish flakes easily with a fork (about 20 to 30 minutes). Remove from baking pan onto serving dish. Garnish with chopped parsley.

Orange-Lemon Marinade

1/3 cup fresh ORANGE JUICE
¼ cup fresh LEMON JUICE
2 tablespoons HONEY
1 teaspoon CURRY POWDER
1/3 cup SALAD OIL
SALT and PEPPER

Combine all ingredients in jar and shake well. Cover and store in refrigerator. Will keep from two to three weeks. Use with plain baked fish, fish sticks, or shrimp salad.

Broiled Fish

2 lbs. FISH
3 slices GRAPEFRUIT (unpeeled)
2 tablespoons PARSLEY (chopped)
½ lb. BUTTER
1 cup GRAPEFRUIT JUICE
SALT and PEPPER
2 teaspoons WORCESTERSHIRE
SAUCE

Prepare fish for broiling and set in shallow baking pan. Place grapefruit slices on fish. Salt and pepper well. Sprinkle with parsley. Dot with butter and place in 350 F oven for 25 minutes. As fish bakes, add 1/3 cup of grapefruit juice. When fish is well cooked, set under broiler flame and brown. Transfer fish to platter. Pour grapefruit juice into saucepan. Add Worcestershire Sauce and any liquid from broiler pan. Bring to a boil. Strain heated sauce over fish and sprinkle with paprika.

Fish Fillets

1 pound FISH FILLETS (fresh or
frozen)
¼ teaspoon SALT
⅛ teaspoon PEPPER
⅛ teaspoon dried leaf OREGANO
3 tablespoons BUTTER (melted)
PAPRIKA
1 GRAPEFRUIT (sectioned)

Place fillets on aluminum foil in broiler pan. Add salt, pepper and oregano to butter. Brush fish with half the mixture. Sprinkle with paprika. Place in preheated broiler about 5 inches below heat. Broil until fish is easily flaked but still moist, about 10 to 12 minutes. Three minutes before fish is cooked, place grapefruit sections on top, brush remaining butter mixture. Contine broiling until fish is easily flaked with fork. (Serves 4)

★ ★ ★

To remove fish, onion, or other odors from hands, pour lemon juice in the palms and rub well.

Citrus Pork Chops

6 PORK CHOPS (½ to ¾ thick)
2 tablespoons LARD
1 teaspoon SALT
⅛ teaspoon PEPPER
½ cup ORANGE JUICE
1 teaspoon LEMON JUICE
2 tablespoons HONEY
¼ teaspoon CINNAMON
¼ teaspoon GINGER
1 teaspoon SUGAR
2 ORANGES (sectioned
FLOUR (for thickening)

Brown chops in lard (or meat drippings). Pour off drippings. Season chops with salt and pepper. Combine juices, honey, spices, and sugar. Pour over chops. Cover tightly and cook slowly 45 minutes (or til done). Add orange sections and cook just until heated through. Remove chops. Thicken pan liquid with flour for gravy and spoon over hot chops.

Spiced Chicken

1½ cups ORANGE SECTIONS
ORANGE JUICE
2 tablespoons BROWN SUGAR
2 tablespoons VINEGAR
1 teaspoon MACE (or nutmeg)
1 teaspoon dried leaf BASIL
1 clove GARLIC (minced)
½ cup FLOUR
1 teaspoon SALT
⅛ teaspoon PEPPER
1 broiler-fryer CHICKEN (in serving pieces)
2 tablespoons SALAD OIL

Drain orange sections and add additional juice to make 1 cup. Combine orange juice, brown sugar, vinegar, mace, basil and garlic in saucepan. Simmer over low heat 10 minutes. Combine flour, salt and pepper. Coat chicken with this mixture. Heat oil in skillet; add chicken pieces and brown on all sides. Add orange sauce. Cover and simmer 30 minutes or until tender. Add orange sections and simmer, covered, 5 minutes longer. (Serves 4)

Orange Barbequed Chicken

1 3-lb. CHICKEN, cut-up
3 to 4 fresh ORANGES
SALT and PEPPER to taste

Wash and cut up fresh chicken and place in large pot. Fill with water to cover. Add dash of salt. Bring to a boil, lower heat and simmer until cooked (but still firm, about 45 minutes). Remove cooked chicken from pot and cool. Place in refrigerator until about 45 minutes before serving. Then set cooled chicken on grill over hot coals. Salt and pepper to taste. Cut one orange in half and squeeze juice over each chicken piece. Turn frequently until light brown and chicken is heated thoroughly. Remove from heat. Cut second orange in half and squeeze juice over chicken. Cut third orange into wedges and serve with chicken.

Fiji Orange Chicken Chunks

6 whole CHICKEN
  BREASTS
1½ teaspoons GARLIC
  SALT
1 teaspoon PAPRIKA
¼ cup SALAD OIL
1 can (9 oz.) PINEAPPLE
  CHUNKS
1¼ cups CHICKEN
  BROTH
¼ cup WINE VINEGAR
½ cup CELERY (sliced)

1 small GREEN PEPPER
  (¼ inch strips)
1 large ONION (sliced)
1 large TOMATO (cut into
  wedges)
1 tablespoon SOY SAUCE
3 tablespoons DARK
  BROWN SUGAR
2 tablespoons
  CORNSTARCH
½ cup WATER
3 ORANGES (sectioned)

Bone and skin chicken breasts and cut into two-inch pieces. Sprinkle chicken with garlic salt and paprika. Heat oil in large skillet; add chicken and cook about 5 minutes, until white. Add syrup from pineapple, chicken broth and vinegar. Cover and simmer 10 minutes. Add celery, green pepper and onion. Cover and cook 5 minutes longer. Add tomato wedges and drained pineapple chunks. Blend soy sauce, brown sugar, cornstarch and water. Add to sauce and cook, stirring constantly, until mixture thickens and comes to a boil; cook 1 minute longer. Add orange sections and toss lightly. Serve over fried rice. (Serves 6)

Orange Fried Chicken

1/3 cup FLOUR
1 teaspoon SALT
¼ teaspoon PEPPER
1 (2½ to 3-lb.) frying CHICKEN, cut-up
Cooking OIL
1 fresh ORANGE

Combine flour, salt and pepper in paper or plastic bag. Shake several pieces of chicken in bag to coat with flour mixture. Heat 1/4 inch of oil in large, heavy skillet. Cut whole orange into quarters and add to oil. Lightly brown chicken on all sides for 15 to 20 minutes. Cover tightly and cook over low heat about 20 to 30 minutes (or until tender). Remove cover and cook about 10 minutes more. When serving add fresh grated orange peel, if desired.

Lemon Lamb
with Potatoes

1 LEG of young LAMB
3 GARLIC CLOVES
SALT and PEPPER
4 tablespoons BUTTER (melted)
JUICE Of 1 LEMON
20 small POTATOES (peeled)
SALT
2 tablespoons TOMATO PASTE
2 cups HOT WATER

Wash leg of lamb. Slit with sharp knife in various places on both sides. Slice garlic thinly and insert slices in slits. Season with salt and pepper and brush with melted butter. Squeeze lemon juice over lamb and place meat in roasting pan, fat side up.

While lamb is browning in a 450 F oven, sprinkle potatoes with salt. Then rub potatoes with tomato paste and let stand for a few minutes. Add potatoes to the baking pan with the water and reduce oven heat to 350 F. Turn and baste potatoes occasionally during roasting. When lamb is done (about three hours roasting), remove to heated platter to keep warm. Increase oven temperature to 425 F and brown potatoes for 20 minutes more (Serves 8)

Basic Citrus Stuffing

2 cups BREAD CRUMBS
2 slices BACON (chopped fine)
RIND of 2 ORANGES (grated)
1 tablespoon LEMON RIND (grated)
Pinch of THYME
SALT and PEPPER
1 ONION (chopped)
2 APPLES (diced)
2 EGGS

Combine the ingredients in the order given and stuff poultry. Stuffing may also be baked separately for 30 to 40 minutes.

Lemony Wings

3 lbs. CHICKEN WINGS
½ cup HONEY
3 tablespoons CORNSTARCH
½ teaspoon GINGER
1 teaspoon SALT
¼ teaspoon PEPPER
¾ cup COLD WATER
1/3 cup LEMON JUICE
¼ cup SOY SAUCE

Clip wing tips. Place wings in single layer in baking pan in 400 F oven for 10 minutes. Turn wings once. Combine all other ingredients in saucepan in order listed, stirring to make smooth mixture. Heat, stirring constantly, until mixture thickens and comes to a boil. Boil three minutes. Brush mixture over roasted wings and continue baking, turning and glazing until wings are tender.

Citrus Marinade

¾ cup OIL
¼ cup SOY SAUCE
½ cup WHITE WINE
JUICE of 1 LEMON
2 cloves GARLIC (crushed)
½ teaspoon Powdered GINGER
1 teaspoon BROWN SUGAR

Combine all ingredients and use as marinade for meats.

Crown Roast of Pork Valencia

6 to 7 lb. CROWN ROAST of PORK
SALT and PEPPER
1 lb. Bulk PORK SAUSAGE
1 cup ONION (chopped)
1 cup RICE (pre-cooked)
½ cup ORANGE JUICE

1 tablespoon PARSLEY FLAKES
½ teaspoon POULTRY SEASONING
4 ORANGES (sectioned)
½ cup RAISINS
½ cup PECANS (chopped)

Sprinkle roast with salt and pepper. Place on rack in shallow roasting pan, with rib ends up. Fill center cavity with crumpled aluminum foil to keep crown shape. Cover rib ends with foil. Roast in 350 F oven 35 to 40 minutes per pound (meat thermometer 185 F).

Meanwhile, break up sausage in large skillet and cook wtih onion until meat is done and onion is golden. Add rice, orange juice, parsley and poultry seasoning. Cover and simmer 5 minutes. Add orange sections, raisins and pecans. Mix lightly and store in refrigerator.

An hour before end of roasting time, remove roast from oven. Remove foil; fill cavity with stuffing mixture, piling high in the center. Return to oven and roast one hour more. Serve with Valencia Sauce. (Serves 8)

Valencia Sauce

3 tablespoons PORK DRIPPINGS
3 tablespoons FLOUR
2 cups ORANGE JUICE
¾ teaspoon SALT
¼ teaspoon POULTRY SEASONING
1 ORANGE (sectioned)

Blend together pan drippings and flour in roasting pan. Gradually stir in orange juice; add seasoning. Stir constantly over medium heat until mixture thickens and comes to a boil. Stir in brown particles from bottom of pan. Add orange sections and heat. Serve with crown roast of pork. (About 2 cups)

Mixed Grill

For each portion:
1 LAMB CHOP
1 slice BACON
1 SAUSAGE LINK
½ GRAPEFRUIT
Portions of Shoe-String POTATOES

Broil lamb chops, bacon and sausage. To broil grapefruit, sprinkle with cinnamon and brown sugar, dot with butter and broil 10 minutes.

To serve grill: put strip of bacon and sausage across lamp chop on platter. Add broiled grapefruit and potatoes. Garnish with parsley.

Sun Belt Lasagne

1 pound PORK (ground)
½ cup ONION (chopped)
1 clove GARLIC (minced)
3 tablespoons FLOUR
1½ cups ORANGE JUICE
1¼ teaspoons SALT, (divided)
½ teaspoon SUGAR
¼ teaspoon PEPPER (divided)
¼ teaspoon rubbed SAGE
¼ teaspoon CINNAMON
4 ounces LASAGNA NOODLES (cooked)
1 pound (2 cups) CREAMED COTTAGE CHEESE
1 EGG (beaten)
¼ cup PARSLEY (chopped)
½ teaspoon ORANGE RIND (grated)

In large skillet break up pork with fork. Stir over medium heat until browned. Add onion and garlic and cook until tender. Blend in flour. Stir in orange juice, 1 teaspoon salt, sugar, 1/8 teaspoon pepper, sage and cinnamon. Cook until mixture thickens and comes to a boil. Remove from heat. In medium bowl mix cottage cheese, egg, parsley, orange rind, remaining 1/4 teaspoon salt and 1/8 teaspoon pepper.

Place a layer of half of cooked lasagna noodles on bottom of 11x7 baking dish. Spoon half of cheese mixture over noodles, spoon half of pork mixture over cheese, then repeat with remaining lasagna noodles, cottage cheese and pork mixture. Bake uncovered in 350 F oven 30 minutes. Garnish with orange slices. (Serves 6)

Citrus Ham Balls

2 EGGS
½ cup ORANGE JUICE
3 cups fine soft BREAD CRUMBS
2 cups ground cooked HAM
1 tablespoon ONION (minced)
¼ cup PARSLEY (chopped)
½ teaspoon ORANGE RIND (grated)
¼ teaspoon DRY MUSTARD
½ teaspoon dried leaf SAGE
2 tablespoons BUTTER
Hot cooked RICE

Beat eggs in medium bowl. Add orange juice and bread crumbs. Mix well and let stand 5 minutes. Add ham, onion, parsley, orange rind, dry mustard and sage and mix well. Shape into 18 meatballs about 1 inch in diameter. Heat butter in skillet, add meatballs and brown lightly on all sides. Add to Citrus Sauce. Serve with hot cooked rice. (Serves 4)

Citrus Sauce

3 tablespoons CORNSTARCH
3 cups ORANGE JUICE
3 tablespoons SUGAR
½ teaspoon ONION (minced)
¾ teaspoon SALT
½ teaspoon DRY MUSTARD
½ teaspoon dried leaf SAGE
¼ teaspoon GINGER
1 teaspoon VINEGAR
¼ teaspoon PEPPER
1 cup RAISINS
2 ORANGES (sectioned)

Blend cornstarch with a small amount of the orange juice in a saucepan. Add remaining orange juice, sugar, onion, salt, dry mustard, sage, ginger, vinegar, pepper and raisins. Mix well and cook, stirring constantly, until mixture thickens and comes to a boil. Add orange sections.

Ham a la Orange

1 (5-lb.) cooked HAM
1 cup ORANGE JUICE
½ cup dark CORN SYRUP
¼ teaspoon CLOVES

Set ham on rack in shallow baking pan. Combine orange juice, syrup and cloves and mix well. Spoon part of glaze over ham. Bake in 325 F oven, basting frequently with glaze. Bake until meat thermometer reaches 140 F (about 1½ hours). Remove ham from pan and spoon pan drippings over meat.

Grapefruit Croquettes

½ cup FLOUR (sifted)
1 teaspoon BAKING POWDER
¼ teaspoon NUTMEG (ground)
¼ teaspoon CINNAMON
1 EGG (lightly beaten)
1 cup GRAPEFRUIT PIECES
1½ cups HAM (ground, fully cooked)

Sift together dry ingredients. Add egg and grapefruit pieces. (Grapefruit must be well drained.) Mix well. Fold in ham. Drop by tablespoonfuls into deep hot fat. Fry one minute (or til deep golden brown on all sides). Drain and serve with warmed syrup to which grapefruit pieces have been added.

Glazed Ham Steak

1 Center Cut HAM STEAK
1/3 cup SUGAR
¼ cup HONEY
1½ tablespoons GRAPEFRUIT PEEL
   (grated)
¼ cup GRAPEFRUIT JUICE

Score steak 1/8-inch deep in a diamond pattern on both sides. Place in shallow baking pan. In a saucepan, combine the remaining ingredients and bring to a boil. Cook 2 to 3 minutes, until slightly thickened. Pour glaze over ham. Cover with aluminum foil and bake in 325 F oven for 30 minutes. Remove foil and bake for 25 minutes longer. Serve with sauce.

Saucy Pork Chops

2 lbs. PORK CHOPS (1-inch thick)
1 LEMON
¾ cup ORANGE JUICE
½ cup SHERRY
1 teaspoon BROWN SUGAR
¾ teaspoon SALT
1 clove GARLIC (crushed)
½ cup OLIVES (pitted, drained)
1 ONION (sliced)

Trim chops and render in frypan. Remove trimmings and brown chops slowly. Cut thin slices from lemon (about 5 slices) and extract juice from remaining lemon to measure one tablespoon. Combine juice with orange juice, sherry, brown sugar, salt, and garlic. Turn meat and top each chop with lemon slice. Sprinkle olives and onion rings over chops. Pour juice-sherry mixture over chops and heat to boiling. Cover pan, and simmer 30 minutes, til tender. Transfer meat to serving platter. Skim off excess fat from sauce, pour over chops and serve at once. (Serves 4)

Citrus Spareribs

4 to 5 lbs. SPARERIBS
1 can (6 oz.) ORANGE JUICE (frozen
    concentrate, thawed, undiluted)
¾ cup KETCHUP
2 tablespoons MOLASSES
1 teaspoon WORCESTERSHIRE
    SAUCE
½ teaspoon TABASCO SAUCE
2 teaspoons SALT
4 teaspoons ONION (grated)

Place spareribs (cut in serving pieces) in large pot. Cover with water and bring to a boil. Reduce heat and simmer (covered) 30 minutes. Drain and refrigerate until ready to grill.

Mix orange concentrate with remaining ingredients. Place spare ribs on grill set about 8 inches from heat. Cook 15 minutes. Turn and brush with orange sauce. Cook 15 to 30 minutes longer, turning and brushing frequently with sauce. (Serves 4 to 6)

Citrus-Glazed Lamb Roast

5 lb. LEG OF LAMB
SALT and PEPPER
2 tablespoons CORNSTARCH
1 teaspoon CINNAMON
¼ teaspoon GINGER
2 cups ORANGE JUICE
2 tablespoons HONEY
2 GRAPEFRUITS (sectioned)
1 ORANGE (sectioned)

Set leg of lamb on rack in shallow roasting pan. Rub with salt and pepper. In a saucepan, blend cornstarch, cinnamon and ginger. Slowly stir orange juice and honey into cornstarch mixture. Cook over low heat, stirring constantly until thick and clear. Remove from heat and pour one cup of sauce over lamb.

To remaining orange juice add sectioned grapefruits and orange. Roast lamb at 325 F for 3 hours, basting frequently. Heat reserved sauce, stirring slowly and serve with lamb. (Serves 8)

Grapefruit Sausage Kraut

1 tablespoon SALAD OIL
1 ONION (chopped)
1½ pounds SWEET SAUSAGE
1 green CABBAGE (shredded)
2 teaspoons SUGAR
2 teaspoons DILL SEED
½ teaspoon SALT
1½ cups GRAPEFRUIT JUICE
2 GRAPEFRUITS (sectioned)

Heat oil in large saucepan or Dutch oven. Add onion and cook until tender, but not brown. Cut sausage into 1-inch pieces. Add to pan and cook until browned on all sides. Add shredded cabbage. Cover and cook until cabbage begins to wilt (about 10 minutes). Sprinkle with sugar, dill seed and salt and add grapefruit juice. Cover and cook over medium heat 10 minutes. Remove cover, stir and continue to cook over low heat, uncovered, 20 minutes. Stir occasionally. Add grapefruit sections and heat. (Serves 6)

Orange Pot Roast

1 tablespoon SALAD OIL
1 (5-to 6-lb.) boneless
   RUMP ROAST
2 teaspoons SALT
¼ teaspoon PEPPER
1 ONION (sliced)
1 BAY LEAF
1 tablespoon BROWN
   SUGAR
½ teaspoon dried leaf
   THYME
1 teaspoon ORANGE RIND
   (grated)
2 cups ORANGE JUICE
2 tablespoons
   GRAPEFRUIT JUICE
1½ tablespoons FLOUR

In large Dutch oven heat oil. Brown roast on all sides. Add all remaining ingredients except flour, cover and bake in 350 F oven 3 hours (or until meat is tender). Remove meat to platter and keep warm. Stir a little of the liquid into the flour to make a smooth paste. Stir paste into liquid in pan and cook over medium heat, stirring constantly, until gravy thickens slightly. Simmer 2 minutes. Slice meat and serve with gravy. (Serves 12)

Liver with Orange Sauce

2 tablespoons BUTTER
½ ONION (sliced)
4 slices CALF LIVER
SALT and PEPPER
2/3 cup ORANGE JUICE
2 teaspoons CORNSTARCH
3 ORANGES (sectioned)

Heat butter in pan. Add onion and cool until tender (but not brown). Sprinkle liver with salt and pepper and brown quickly on both sides in pan. Add juice to pan and simmer, covered, until meat is tender (about 8 to 10 minutes). Remove liver to serving plate.

Blend cornstarch with one tablespoon cold water. Add to pan liquid and cook, stirring constantly, until mixture thickens and comes to a boil. Add orange sections and stir over low heat until orange is heated. Spoon sauce over meat. (Serves 4)

Hawaiian Kabobs

½ cup BUTTER
¼ cup PINEAPPLE JUICE
2 tablespoons LEMON JUICE
3 tablespoons BROWN SUGAR
⅛ teaspoon CLOVES (ground)
⅛ teaspoon DRY MUSTARD
1 lb. Cooked HAM CHUNKS
   (1-inch x ½-inch)
1 can (13 oz.) PINEAPPLE CHUNKS
   (drained)
1 ORANGE (sectioned)

Melt butter in saucepan. Add pineapple and lemon juices, brown sugar, and cloves and mustard. Cook and stir until thoroughly heated. Thread ham, pineapple and orange sections on skewers. Place on broiler pan and spoon butter sauce over kabobs while broiling. Broil five minutes. Turn kabobs once. Serve over rice.

Lemony Chops

2 lbs. LAMB (or pork) CHOPS
2 LEMONS (unpeeled, sliced)
1 ONION (sliced)
1 GREEN PEPPER (sliced)
1 teaspoon SALT
2 cups TOMATO JUICE
Pats of BUTTER

Place chops in large pan. Cover meat with sliced lemon, onion, and pepper. Sprinkle salt over all, pour in tomato juice, and dot with butter pats. Cover tightly and cook for 1½ hours (or until thoroughly cooked). (Serves 6)

VEGETABLES

Squash in Orange Cream Sauce

1 lb. Yellow SQUASH
1 lb. ZUCCHINI
2 tablespoons frozen ORANGE JUICE
concentrate (thawed, undiluted)
2 tablespoons BUTTER (melted)
1 cup SOUR CREAM
2 tablespoons FLOUR
Sprigs of PARSLEY

Scrub squash. Cut slice from stem and blossom ends, but do not peel. Cut into thin slices. Place in small amount of boiling salted water. Cover and cook about 10 minutes.

To prepare sauce, stir orange concentrate into melted butter and heat until just warm. Combine sour cream and flour and stir into sauce. Heat, but do not boil.

To serve, pour heated sauce over cooked squash slices. Garnish with parsley. (Makes 4 servings)

Carrots in Orange Glaze

1 bunch CARROTS
2 tablespoons FLOUR
2 tablespoons SUGAR
¼ teaspoon SALT
Dash PAPRIKA
2 tablespoons BUTTER
¼ cup COLD WATER
½ cup ORANGE JUICE
2 tablespoons LEMON JUICE

Cook carrots cut into 1-inch slices and set aside. Prepare glaze by mixing flour, sugar, salt and paprika. Add butter, cold water, orange juice, and lemon juice and cook in top of double boiler over boiling water five minutes until thickened, stirring occasionally. Put cooked carrots in a skillet. Pour sauce over carrots and cook slowly until thoroughly glazed, stirring constantly.

Orange-Banana Yams

1 (23-oz.) can WHOLE SWEET
  POTATOES (in heavy syrup)
1 tablespoon CORNSTARCH
1/3 cup firmly packed LIGHT
  BROWN SUGAR
1 cup ORANGE JUICE
1 tablespoon BUTTER
1 tablespoon ORANGE RIND
  (grated)
3 medium BANANAS

Drain sweet potatoes and save syrup for other use. Slice potatoes in half lengthwise. Place in a single layer in an oblong glass 1½-quart baking dish.

Stir together cornstarch and brown sugar in small saucepan. Gradually stir in orange juice, keeping smooth. Stir constantly over moderate heat until clear and thickened. Remove from heat. Stir in butter and orange rind.

Peel bananas. Score by drawing a fork lengthwise down sides. Slice crosswise about one-fourth-inch thick. Arrange bananas over sweet potatoes. Spoon orange sauce evenly over top, so yams—and especially the bananas—are covered with it.

Bake in preheated 400 F oven until bubbling hot (15 to 20 minutes). Serve at once. (Serves 6)

Grapefruit Harvard Beets

1 can BEETS
2 tablespoons SUGAR
1 tablespoon CORNSTARCH
¼ teaspoon SALT
¼ cup GRAPEFRUIT JUICE
2 cups GRAPEFRUIT SECTIONS

Use either tiny whole or sliced beets. Drain and save beet juice. Combine sugar, cornstarch and salt in saucepan. Combine beet juice and grapefruit juice and add to starch mixture in saucepan. Cook over medium heat, stirring constantly, until mixture comes to a boil. Boil half a minute and add drained beets. Heat to serving temperature. Remove from heat. Add drained grapefruit sections, broken into small pieces. Serve hot.

Marinated Broccoli

1 GRAPEFRUIT
2 lbs. BROCCOLI (fresh)
1 cup bottled ITALIAN DRESSING
¼ cup GRAPEFRUIT JUICE
¼ cup BLACK OLIVES (pitted, sliced)

Peel and section grapefruit and reserve juice. Drain and refrigerate grapefruit sections. Clean and trim broccoli. Cook broccoli until tender (about 10 minutes). Drain carefully and place in shallow glass dish. Combine reserved juice with Italian dressing and grapefruit juice. Pour over hot broccoli. Cover and chill about 2 to 3 hours.

When ready to serve, arrange chilled broccoli spears on dish and add grapefruit sections. Garnish with black olives. (Serves 4)

Orange Rice

½ cup ONIONS (chopped)
2 tablespoons BUTTER
5 tablespoons frozen ORANGE
    JUICE concentrate
2 tablespoons dry VERMOUTH
1 teaspoon SALT
¼ teaspoon BLACK PEPPER
¼ teaspoon CINNAMON
3 cups hot cooked RICE

Cook onions in butter until tender. Add orange juice concentrate, vermouth and seasonings. Heat thoroughly. Pour over hot rice and toss lightly until well blended. Allow to stand 10 minutes so flavors will blend. (Serves 6)

Grapefruit Dip

1 cup SOUR CREAM
1 tablespoon HONEY
JUICE of 1 GRAPEFRUIT

Combine ingredients and mix together until smooth and creamy. Serve in a bowl surrounded by crackers and fresh vegetables for dipping.

Autumn Baked Squash

3 ACORN SQUASH
6 tablespoons BROWN SUGAR
3 tablespoons BUTTER
1 tablespoon grated ORANGE PEEL
3 medium ORANGES (sectioned)

Wash squash, cut in half, and remove seeds. Place cut side down in shallow baking pan. Bake in 375 F oven 40 minutes. Turn cut side up and fill each cavity with 1 tablespoon brown sugar, 1/2 tablespoon butter, 1/2 teaspoon grated peel, and several orange sections. Add water to baking pan, if necessary. Continue baking until tender. Baste occasionally as butter melts and juice forms.

Slivers of Gold Broccoli

1 lb. fresh BROCCOLI
1 fresh LEMON
BUTTER to taste

Wash and clean broccoli. Cut broccoli into flower sections. Cut lemon in half and squeeze the juice. Set juice to one side. With scissors, cut lemon halves into quarters, then into lengthwise strips. Place broccoli into saucepan, add water to cover, dashes of salt, one teaspoon of fresh lemon juice and several slivers of the lemon peel. Cover and bring to boil. Lower heat and simmer until broccoli is tender. Garnish with remaining slivers of lemon and dot with butter when serving.

Citrus Sweet Potato Bake

4 large SWEET POTATOES
WATER to cover
1 teaspoon SALT
1/3 cup SUGAR
1¾ teaspoons
  PUMPKIN PIE SPICE
1½ teaspoons PEEL (orange
  or grapefruit or
  lemon) grated
¼ cup BUTTER
  (or margarine)
1½ cups MILK
2 EGGS (lightly beaten)

Wash sweet potatoes, place in saucepan, cover with water, add several dashes salt, cover and bring to boil. Continue boiling until potatoes are tender. Peel and mash potatoes while hot.

Add remaining ingredients. Pour into buttered one-quart casserole. Bake in preheated 300 F oven 1 1/2 hours (or until a knife inserted in the center comes out clean). Serve at once.

Grapefruit Pilaf

1 package (8 oz.) WHEAT PILAF
1 cup GRAPEFRUIT JUICE
1½ cups WATER
½ cup PARSLEY (chopped)
¼ teaspoon dried leaf THYME
2 cans (7 oz. each) TUNA
1 pkg. (10 oz.) frozen chopped
   BROCCOLI, (thawed and drained)
1 cup GRAPEFRUIT (sections)

In large casserole or Dutch oven, mix together wheat pilaf, grapefruit juice, water, parsley and thyme. Cover and bake in 350 F oven 30 minutes. Stir in tuna, broccoli and grapefruit sections, cover and bake 10 minutes longer. Garnish with additional grapefruit sections. (Serves 4)

Lemon Pilaf

1 cup CELERY (sliced)
1 cup GREEN ONIONS (chopped with
   tops)
2 tablespoons BUTTER
3 cups RICE (cooked)
1 tablespoon LEMON RIND (grated)
1 teaspoon SALT
¼ teaspoon PEPPER

Saute celery and onions in butter til tender. Add rice, lemon rind and seasonings and toss lightly. Continue cooking over low heat (about 2 minutes) til thoroughly heated, stirring occasionally.

Gold Nugget Zucchini

3 to 4 lbs. ZUCCHINI
1 tablespoon SALT
¼ cup BUTTER
2 tablespoons instant
   Minced ONIONS
½ teaspoon fresh
   LEMON PEEL (grated)
3 tablespoons fresh
   LEMON JUICE

Wash zucchini and slice. Place in frypan, adding water to cover. Add dashes of salt, cover and bring to a boil. Continue boiling until tender-crisp stage. Drain.

In a saucepan, melt butter with onions, lemon peel and juice. Pour over drained squash, mix and serve.

Sweet Potato Casserole

2 cups mashed SWEET
   POTATOES
3 tablespoons BUTTER
   (melted)
2 tablespoons WHITE
   SUGAR

1 tablespoon SALT
1 EGG (well beaten)
½ cup HOT MILK
½ cup MARSHMALLOWS
1 GRAPEFRUIT
   (sectioned)
¼ cup BROWN SUGAR

Combine all ingredients (EXCEPT marshmallows, grapefruit and brown sugar) in a greased baking dish. Top wtih marshmallows, grapefruit sections, and sprinkle with brown sugar. Bake in 350 F oven about 30 minutes, until browned.

Grapefruit Corn Relish

4 GRAPEFRUIT
2 cans (12 oz. each) WHOLE KERNEL
   CORN (drained)
1 jar (9¾ oz.) SWEET PICKLE RELISH
2 tablespoons PIMIENTO (chopped)
½ cup SALAD OIL
SALAD GREENS

Cut grapefruits in half. Remove core. Cut around each section, loosening fruit from membrane. Lift fruit out and reserve. Pull out remaining membrane and reserve cups. In medium bowl, mix together grapefruit sections and remaining ingredients. Chill. Spoon into grapefruit shells lined with salad greens to serve. (Serves 8)

Grapefruit Fritters

GRAPEFRUIT SECTIONS
1 EGG WHITE
1 EGG YOLK
1 tablespoon FLOUR
¼ teaspoon SALT
¼ teaspoon BAKING POWDER
1 teaspoon SUGAR

Peel, remove membrane, drain and dry the desired quantity of grapefruit sections. Dip into following batter: beat egg white until stiff. Fold into well-beaten egg yolk. Sift remaining dry ingredients into egg. Fry in smallest amount of fat it is possible to use. Brown quickly. Serve with vegetables or as garnish around meat.

45

DESSERTS

Orange Almond Blancmange

2 envelopes unflavored GELATIN
1½ cups ORANGE JUICE (divided)
1 cup SUGAR
2 cups HEAVY CREAM
1 cup ALMONDS (whole or slivered)

Blanch almonds and grind fine. In medium saucepan sprinkle gelatin over one cup orange juice. Cook over low heat and stir constantly until gelatin dissolves (about 3 minutes). Remove from heat. Stir in sugar and remaining 1/2 cup orange juice. Cool. Stir in heavy cream and almonds. Turn into 4-cup mold and chill until firm. Unmold and garnish with orange sections and whole almonds. (Serves 8)

Orange Blossom Bowl

1 pint HEAVY CREAM
2 tablespoons HONEY
6 tablespoons Frozen ORANGE
    JUICE Concentrate (thawed,
    undiluted)
12 double LADYFINGERS
1 ORANGE (sectioned)

Whip cream in large bowl. Fold in honey and undiluted orange juice. Split ladyfingers and line bottom and sides of glass serving dish. Pour cream mixture into dish. Chill for at least four hours before serving. (Serves 8)

Orange Cream

6 EGG YOLKS
3 EGG WHITES
1 cup SUGAR
2 cups ORANGE JUICE (strained)

In top of a double boiler beat egg yolks and whites until fluffy and light. Continue beating, adding sugar gradually. Fold in orange juice and cook over boiling water until thickened. Pour into serving dish and refrigerate. (Must be served very cold. Serves 4)

Sunshine Ambrosia

3 GRAPEFRUIT (sectioned)
4 ORANGES (sectioned)
1 pint STRAWBERRIES (washed,
    hulled and halved)
¾ cup FLAKED COCONUT
1/3 cup SUGAR

To section grapefruit and oranges, cut slice from top, then cut off peel in strips from top to bottom, cutting deep enough to remove white membrane, then cut slice from bottom. (Or cut off peel round and round in spiral fashion.) Remove any remaining white membrane. Cut along side of each dividing membrane from outside to middle of core. Remove section by section over bowl to retain juice from fruit.

Layer grapefruit sections, orange sections and strawberries in bowl. Sprinkle each layer with coconut and sugar. (Serves 8)

Southern Ambrosia

6 to 8 ORANGES (peeled and
    sectioned)
1 can COCONUT FLAKES
CUSTARD SAUCE

Chill oranges, coconut flakes and sauce separately and serve in individual dishes in layers--custard, orange sections, coconut, etc.

Custard Sauce

1 cup MILK
1 cup HEAVY CREAM
4 EGG YOLKS
¼ cup SUGAR
1 tablespoon FLOUR
¼ teaspoon SALT
¾ teaspoon RUM FLAVORING

Heat milk and cream in double boiler in top, until tiny bubbles form around the edge. Remove from heat and set aside. Beat eggs slightly in mixing bowl and add dry ingredients. Mix thoroughly and add very slowly to hot mixture, stirring constantly. Return to double boiler and cook until thick as heavy cream. Chill and add flavoring before serving.

47

Jellied Ambrosia

1 tablespoon Unflavored GELATIN
¼ cup SUGAR
½ cup COLD WATER
1¼ cups ORANGE JUICE
1 tablespoon LEMON JUICE
2 ORANGES
1 BANANA
¼ cup COCONUT (flaked)

Mix gelatin and sugar in saucepan. Add cold water. Stir over low heat til dissolved. Add orange and lemon juice. Chill til partially set. Peel and segment oranges. Cut in pieces, reserving a few whole segments for garnish.

Fold orange slices, cut-up bananas and coconut into gelatin. Pour into 4½ cup mold and chill until firm. Unmold and garnish with orange segments.

Apricot Grapefruit Ice

1 can APRICOT NECTAR
1 cup POWDERED SUGAR
2 cups GRAPEFRUIT (peeled
    segments)

Break segments into small pieces in bowl. Add nectar. Add sugar and stir until dissolved. Pour into refrigerator freezing tray and freeze about two hours. Stir and continue freezing about two hours. (Makes 1 quart)

Candied Orange Slices

1 lb. SUGAR
1 pint WATER
ORANGES

Peel and quarter oranges. Make a syrup of sugar and water. Let syrup boil until it will harden in water. Remove from fire and dip quarters of orange in syrup. Let orange quarters drain over sieve until cool, when sugar will crystallize.

★ ★ ★

Scissors are preferable to a knife when cutting citrus peel.

48

Citrus Sundae

2 cup ORANGE SECTIONS (or
 tangerine sections) drained
¼ cup orange-flavored LIQUEUR
1 pt. vanilla ICE CREAM
1 pt. orange SHERBET

In a shallow leakproof covered container, marinate the orange or tangerine sections in the liqueur for a day. Turn container upside down once during the period.

At serving time, scoop a ball of ice cream and one of sherbet into each individual serving dish. Top with oranges and marinade. (Serves 6)

Lemon Snow

1 tablespoon unflavored GELATIN
¼ cup COLD WATER
1 cup BOILING WATER
¾ cup SUGAR
¼ teaspoon SALT
¼ cup LEMON JUICE
2 EGGS (separated)

Soften gelatin in cold water. Add boiling water, sugar and salt. Stir until dissolved. Add lemon juice and chill until partially set. Beat egg whites until stiff and add to mixture. Beat until stiff. Pour into 1½ quart mold and chill until firm. (Serve with Lemon Sauce.)

Lemon Sauce

1 tablespoon CORNSTARCH (level)
½ cup SUGAR
1 teaspoon LEMON RIND (grated)
1 cup COLD WATER
2 tablespoons LEMON JUICE
2 tablespoons BUTTER
¼ cup MARSHMALLOW BITS
Dash SALT

Mix cornstarch with sugar, lemon rind and cold water. Bring to a boil and boil five minutes. Remove from heat. Add lemon juice, butter, marshmallows and salt, stirring until sauce is clear.

49

Frozen Orange Cream

1 tablespoon unflavored GELATIN
½ cup ORANGE JUICE
3 tablespoons ORANGE RIND
  (grated)
1 tablespoon LEMON JUICE
2/3 cup SUGAR
1 cup BUTTERMILK
1 cup WHIPPING CREAM (whipped)

Dissolve gelatin in orange juice over low heat. Remove from heat and combine with remaining ingredients EXCEPT whipped cream. Chill until partially set. Fold in whipped cream. Pour into refrigerator tray and freeze until firm. (Serves 6)

Orange Bavarian Cream

1 tablespoon unflavored GELATIN
¼ cup COLD WATER
¾ cup ORANGE JUICE
2 tablespoons LEMON JUICE
½ teaspoon ORANGE RIND (grated)
1/3 cup SUGAR
¼ teaspoon SALT
1 cup WHIPPING CREAM
1 cup fresh ORANGE SECTIONS
  (cut in pieces)

Soften gelatin in water and set aside. Combine fruit juices, orange rind, sugar, and salt. Heat to simmering. Dissolve gelatin in hot mixture. Chill until mixture begins to thicken.

Whip cream only until stiff. Fold cream and orange sections into gelatin mixture. Pour into a one-quart mold and chill until firm.

Grapefruit Meringues

2 GRAPEFRUIT
2 EGG WHITES
½ cup SUGAR

Cut each fruit in half and remove pulp with a sharp knife. Cut pulp into small pieces. Beat egg whites until stiff. Fold in sugar, then fold in grapefruit pieces. Return mixture to the half shells from which membrance has been removed. Bake in 275 F oven for 30 minutes and serve warm. (Serves 4)

Lemon Bavarian Cream

½ cup SUGAR
¼ cup LEMON JUICE
2 EGGS (separated)
½ teaspoon Unflavored GELATIN
1 tablespoon COLD WATER
½ cup HEAVY CREAM

Combine 1/2 the sugar and lemon juice in top of double boiler. Heat slowly. Beat egg yolks with remaining sugar. Pour heated juice over yolks. Return mixture to pan and cook, stirring constantly, until thickened. Remove from heat.

Soak gelatin in cold water and add to pan, stirring occasionally until cooled. Beat egg whites until stiff and fold in. Beat cream until stiff and fold in. Pour into mold, chill, and serve.

Lemon-Chocolate Mousse

4 oz. CHOCOLATE (cooking, sweet)
1 teaspoon BUTTER
5 EGG YOLKS
1½ tablespoons LEMON JUICE
2½ teaspoons LEMON RIND (grated)
2 tablespoons SUGAR

In top of double boiler, melt the chocolate and butter. Remove from heat and cool. Beat egg yolks until thick. Beat in lemon juice, lemon rind and sugar. Add the cooled melted chocolate. Pour into eight individual cups, chill until set (at least four hours). Serve with shaved chocolate and grated lemon rind. (Serves 8)

Honey Grapefruit Mousse

2 GRAPEFRUIT
1 teaspoon GELATIN
1 tablespoon COLD WATER
¾ cup HONEY
2 cups HEAVY CREAM

Peel grapefruit, section and cut into small pieces. Soften gelatin for 5 minutes in cold water. Heat the honey and add gelatin, stirring until dissolved. Add grapefruit, remove from fire, and when cold add cream beaten stiff. Pour into freezer tray and place in the freezing compartment of refrigerator.

Lemon Sherbet

1½ tablespoons GELATIN
2 tablespoons COLD WATER
¾ cup LEMON JUICE
1 cup SUGAR
3 tablespoons LEMON RIND (grated)
½ teaspoon VANILLA
1¼ cups MILK
1 EGG WHITE

Soften gelatin in water and set aside. Heat lemon juice and sugar to dissolve the sugar. Pour over gelatin and cool. Add lemon rind and vanilla. Slowly stir in milk. Pour into refrigerator tray and freeze to firm mush. Whip with rotary beater until creamy; fold in egg white and return to refrigerator. Freeze until firm, stirring occasionally. (Serves 6)

Grapefruit Cream Sherbet

2¾ cups GRAPEFRUIT JUICE
2 cups SUGAR
1 tablespoon ORANGE PEEL (grated)
1 teaspoon GRAPEFRUIT PEEL
    (grated)
1½ cups ORANGE JUICE
2 cups HEAVY CREAM
Pinch of SALT
2 EGGS (separated)

Heat grapefruit juice, but do NOT boil. Dissolve 1 1/2 cups sugar in the heated juice. Add peels and orange juice. Pour into freezer tray and freeze to mush.

Beat cream until stiff and to it add remaining 1/2 cup sugar and salt (while beating). Beat egg yolks until thick and lemon colored. Beat whites separately until stiff. Combine yolks and whites with stiff whipped cream. Turn the creamy mixture into frozen mixture in freezer tray and continue freezing.

Baked Grapefruit Alaska

Cut grapefruit in halves crosswise. Cut around each section with a sharp knife. Snip out the center with shears, cutting out more of the center than usual. Sprinkle with sugar.

When ready to serve, spoon two heaping tablespoons of ice cream in the center cavity of each grapefruit. Cover completely with meringue. Bake in 450 F oven long enough to brown and serve immediately.

Orangy Sherbet

4 tablespoons LEMON JUICE (fresh)
1 cup ORANGE JUICE (fresh)
1 cup SUGAR
2 cups MILK

Pour juices over sugar until sugar dissolves. Pour milk into juice and freeze in refrigerator ice cube trays. Do not stir while freezing. (Serves 8)

Orange Fondue

3 tablespoons SUGAR
2 tablespoons CORNSTARCH
¼ teaspoon SALT
2 cups ORANGE JUICE
2 whole CLOVES
1 tablespoon BUTTER
1 tablespoon ORANGE RIND (grated)
½ teaspoon LIME JUICE

Mix sugar, cornstarch and salt in a saucepan or fondue pot. Stir in orange juice and add cloves. Cook over medium heat, stirring constantly, until mixture thickens and comes to a boil. Cook, stirring constantly, 1 minute. Stir in butter, orange rind and lime juice. Keep warm over Sterno canned heat or chafing dish liquid fuel. Serve with pieces of poundcake, ladyfingers, marshmallows, and chocolate cookies. (Makes 2½ cups)

Orange Flummery

4 EGGS (beaten)
1 cup LIGHT CREAM
1 cup ORANGE JUICE
½ teaspoon ORANGE PEEL (grated)
¾ cup SUGAR
⅛ teaspoon NUTMEG
2 teaspoons BUTTER

Combine all ingredients in a saucepan EXCEPT butter. Stir over low heat until mixture thickens (about 6 minutes). Remove from heat and stir in butter. Pour into individual dishes and chill thoroughly. (Serves 4)

Orange Cottage Cheese Parfaits

1½ cups creamed COTTAGE
 CHEESE
2 tablespoons frozen concentrated
 ORANGE JUICE (thawed,
 undiluted)
2 cups chilled ORANGE and
 GRAPEFRUIT SECTIONS
 (drained)

In small bowl mix cottage cheese and orange concentrate. In parfait glasses or other narrow glasses place alternate layers of drained orange and grapefruit sections and cottage cheese mixture, ending with the sections. Chill or serve immediately. (Serves 4)

Orange Jelly Cubes

2 tablespoons unflavored GELATIN
½ cup COLD WATER
½ cup BOILING WATER
½ cup SUGAR
1 cup ORANGE JUICE
3 tablespoons LEMON JUICE

Soak gelatin in cold water for five minutes. Dissolve in boiling water. Add sugar, orange and lemon juices. Pour into mold and chill. Remove from mold and cut in cubes to serve.

Baked Grapefruit

2 cups CORN FLAKES (crushed)
½ cup BROWN SUGAR (firmly packed)
½ teaspoon CINNAMON
¼ cup BUTTER (melted)
2 GRAPEFRUIT

Combine corn flakes, sugar, cinnamon and butter. Halve grapefruit. Core and loosen sections. Top with corn flake mixture. Bake in 400 F oven from 10 to 15 minutes. Serve immediately.

Citrus in a Shell

2 GRAPEFRUIT
2 ORANGES
2 tablespoons LEMON JUICE
4 tablespoons POWDERED SUGAR
4 sprigs MINT

Wash and halve grapefruit. Remove sections and membrane from grapefruit shells. Place shells in iced water to keep firm. Peel and section oranges. Mix with grapefruit and chill. Add lemon juice. Sprinkle with sugar and place in grapefruit shells. Garnish with mint and chill before serving.

Lemon Cake Pudding

4 EGGS (separated)
3 tablespoons BUTTER
1 cup SUGAR
3 tablespoons FLOUR
¼ teaspoon SALT
1/3 cup LEMON JUICE
2 teaspoons LEMON RIND (grated)
1 cup MILK

Beat egg whites til stiff in small bowl and set aside. Using same beaters, cream butter in a larger bowl. Add sugar gradually and beat until light and fluffy. Beat in egg yolks. Stir in flour, salt, lemon juice, and lemon rind. Blend in milk. Fold in beaten whites. Pour into 9x5 loaf pan. Set in large pan with 1 inch of hot water. Bake in 325 F oven 40 minutes. Increase heat to 350 F and bake 10 minutes longer. (Serves 6)

Orange Nut Nibbles

1 cup SUGAR
½ teaspoon NUTMEG
⅛ teaspoon CREAM OF TARTAR
¼ cup ORANGE JUICE
2 cups WALNUTS (shelled)
½ teaspoon ORANGE RIND (grated)

In heavy saucepan combine sugar, nutmeg, cream of tartar and orange juice. Cook, stirring occasionally, to 246 F on candy thermometer or until a little syrup, dropped into cold water, forms a firm ball. Add nuts and orange rind. Stir until nuts are completely coated. Turn out onto a greased baking sheet or waxed paper. With 2 forks QUICKLY separate nuts and cool. (Makes 2 cups)

Cranberry Dip

1 can (16-oz.) jellied CRANBERRY
  SAUCE
2 tablespoons LIME JUICE
¼ cup HONEY

Assorted bite-size fruit pieces—grapes, bananas, pears, melon, apples, pineapple, strawberries, etc.

Press cranberry sauce through a sieve into a bowl. Stir in lime juice and honey. Place bowl in the center of a large platter and arrange fruit around bowl. Spear fruit with skewers, and dunk into cranberry mixture.

Citrus Gels

1 envelope unflavored GELATIN
1¾ cups ORANGE JUICE (divided)
¼ cup SUGAR
1½ cups drained, chilled ORANGE
  and GRAPEFRUIT sections

Sprinkle gelatin over 1/2 cup orange juice in medium saucepan. Place over low heat and stir constantly until gelatin dissolves, about 3 minutes. Remove from heat. Stir in sugar and remaining 1 1/4 cups juice. Chill until consistency of unbeaten egg white. Stir in drained citrus sections and turn into four juice glasses. Chill until set, about 3 hours. (Serves 4)

Candied Orange Peel

½ lb. ORANGE PEEL
1 cup SUGAR
¼ cup LIGHT CORN SYRUP
½ cup WATER
Pinch ground GINGER
Vegetable SHORTENING

With a small paring knife, strip the white membrane from peel and discard. Cut cleaned peel into thin one-inch strips and set aside.

Combine sugar, corn syrup, water and ginger in a small saucepan. Bring mixture to a boil and cook until it reaches 290 F on candy thermometer. Drop strips of peel into syrup and cook 10 minutes (or until skin is slightly transparent). While peel is cooking, rub two cookie sheets with shortening. Drop pieces of peel on sheets. Allow to cool and dry. Store in covered glass jar, and keep in a dry place.

Candied Grapefruit Peel

4 to 5 GRAPEFRUITS
2 teaspoons COARSE SALT (to each
**   quart WATER)**
2 cups SUGAR
1 cup ORANGE JUICE
¼ cup CORN SYRUP

Wash fruit well. Score the peel into fourths and pull off in sections. Remove most of the white pith from peel. Place peel in large saucepan with salted water to cover by a few inches. Bring to a rolling boil. Then drain immediately and rinse with cold water.

Return peel to pan. Cover with water again BUT no salt. Bring to a boil. Boil vigorously for 10 minutes. Repeat process. Rinse peel in cold water until cooled. Pat dry with paper towels. Cut each section of peel into 1/4-inch strips.

In a heavy saucepan, combine sugar, orange juice and corn syrup. Bring mixture to a boil, stirring until sugar is dissolved. Add peel from saucepan and arrange on wire racks to drain and dry. Roll strips in granulated sugar and return to rack to dry several hours more. Roll in sugar again, then allow to dry several hours. Store peel in tightly covered container until ready to serve.

Candied Citrus Peel

2 large ORANGES
3 medium LEMONS
1 large GRAPEFRUIT
4 large TANGERINES

1½ cups SUGAR
½ cup HONEY
1¾ cups boiling WATER
1 cup SUGAR (for rolling)

Wash the fruit. Cut into quarters. Remove pulp. Cut peels into uniform strips (scissors do a fine job). Place cut peel into large saucepan and cover with cold water. Bring to a boil and boil, uncovered, for 10 minutes. Drain.

Repeat boiling process with fresh cold water and boil for another 10 minutes. Drain. Add tangerine peel at this time and repeat boiling process.

In a large saucepan combine sugar, honey and boiling water. Bring to a boil, stirring until sugar is dissolved. Boil one minute. Add cooked peel and simmer until almost all the syrup is absorbed (about 45 minutes). Peel should be semi-transparent. Drain off syrup and store it in refrigerator in covered plastic container.

Place peel in colander and drain about 10 minutes. Sprinkle granulated sugar on board and coat the drained peel by rolling in sugar. Spread coated candied peel out on wax paper to dry. Store in tightly covered container.

The reserved syrup can be used to candy pineapple chunks for homemade fruitcake. Place one can of drained pineapple chunks in syrup and simmer until pineapple is almost transparent. Add a few drops of food color and let pineapple absorb color. Drain thoroughly and coat with sugar.

Lemon Custard Pudding

1 cup SUGAR
3 tablespoon FLOUR
Dash SALT
JUICE and PEEL of 1 fresh LEMON
1 tablespoon BUTTER (melted)
1 cup MILK
2 EGGS (separated)

Mix sugar, flour, salt, grated rind and juice of one lemon. Add butter, milk and slightly beaten egg yolks. Fold in beaten egg whites. Pour mixture into custard cups (or casserole). Set cups in baking pan; add water to baking pan to almost reach rims of cups. Bake in 325 F oven 30 minutes. Test by inserting knife in center of cup. Serve warm or cold.

Citrus Ice Cream

2 tablespoon
unflavored GELATIN
2 cups fresh
ORANGE JUICE
1½ cups MILK
½ cup SUGAR
1/8 teaspoon SALT

4 EGGS (lightly beaten)
½ cup fresh LIME JUICE
1¼ cups light
CORN SYRUP
1 tablespoon EACH
(grated) ORANGE PEEL
and LEMON PEEL

Dissolve gelatin in orange juice. Set aside. In top of double boiler, combine milk, sugar, salt, and lightly beaten eggs. Cook for seven minutes, stirring constantly. Remove from heat.

Add orange-gelatin mixture, lime juice and corn syrup. Stir well. Cool for two hours.

Gently add cream, orange and lemon peel to cooled mixture. Place in ice cream churn and freeze, according to ice cream maker directions. (Makes 1/2 gallon ice cream.)

Peachy-Orange Sherbet

3½ cups fresh PEACH PULP
2¼ cups fresh ORANGE JUICE
¼ cup SUGAR
2 tablespoons fresh LEMON JUICE

Peel and seed peaches. Cut into chunks and whirl in blender until pureed. Mix together the peach puree, orange juice, sugar and lemon juice. Pour mixture into an ice cream churn and freeze according to ice cream maker directions.

Fresh Grapefruit Ice Cream

4 fresh large GRAPEFRUIT
4 cups HEAVY CREAM
2¾ cups SUGAR
2 fresh LEMONS (juiced)

Remove any seeds from citrus. Cut into quarters. Put fruit, pulp and peel through a food chopper. Combine all ingredients. Place mixture in ice cream churn and freeze according to ice cream maker directions. (Makes 1/2 gallon ice cream.)

Golden Orange Ice Cream

1 EGG
¾ cup SUGAR
1 tablespoon FLOUR
1 tablespoon fresh
  ORANGE PEEL (grated)

1/8 teaspoon SALT
½ cup fresh
  ORANGE JUICE
1 tablespoon
  LEMON JUICE
1 cup HEAVY CREAM

Combine in saucepan egg, sugar, flour, orange peel and salt. Mix well. Slowly blend in orange and lemon juice. Bring to a boil, stirring constantly. Cook until slightly thick. Chill thoroughly. Beat cream until thick. Fold into orange mixture.

Spoon into 9x5x3 pan, ice cube tray, or serving dishes. Freeze until firm.

Lime Ice Cream

4 EGGS
1 cup SUGAR
1 cup light CORN SYRUP
½ cup fresh LIME JUICE

2 teaspoons LIME
  PEEL (grated)
¼ teaspoon GREEN
  FOOD COLOR
2 cups LIGHT CREAM
2 cups HEAVY CREAM

Beat eggs and sugar until light colored and sugar is dissolved. Add corn syrup, lime juice, lime peel and food color. In a separate bowl, lightly whip the light and heavy cream together. Add to egg-sugar mixture and mix well. Place mixture into ice cream churn and freeze according to ice cream maker directions. (Makes 1/2 gallon ice cream.)

Lemon Ice Cream

2 cups SUGAR
¼ cup fresh LEMON JUICE
1 tablespoon LEMON PEEL (grated)
5 cups HEAVY CREAM
¼ teaspoon Yellow FOOD COLOR

Combine sugar, lemon juice and peel. Lightly whip cream and add to first mixture. Add food color and mix well.

This mixture can be frozen one of two ways:

(1)   Pour mixture into freezer trays and place in freezing compartment of refrigerator until firm.

(2)   Pour mixture into ice cream churn and freeze according to ice cream maker directions. (Makes 1/2 gallon ice cream.)

Icy Orange Slices

2 tablespoons unflavored GELATIN
4 tablespoons COLD WATER
3 cups ORANGE JUICE
¾ cup SUGAR
2 tablespoons LEMON JUICE
1 cup ORANGE SEGMENTS

Combine gelatin and water and let stand five minutes. Heat one cup of orange juice in top of double boiler. Add gelatin and sugar. Stir until dissolved and cool. Add remainder of orange juice and lemon juice and chill for several hours, stirring occasionally. Add orange segments and serve ice cold.

Citrus Cup

2 GRAPEFRUIT
4 ORANGES
3 TANGERINES
BRANDY
SUGAR

Peel fruit, discard membranes and pits, and dice. Pour enough brandy over fruit to suit taste and sprinkle with sugar to sweeten.

Lemon Taffy

2 cups SUGAR
¼ cup fresh LEMON JUICE
2 tablespoons BUTTER (or margarine)
¼ cup WATER

Put all ingredients into saucepan and bring to a boil, stirring constantly. Wash down sugar crystals. Continue boiling without stirring, until candy thermometer registers 280 F (or drop a small drop of mixture into ice water. The mixture should separate into hard and brittle threads.).

Pour onto greased cookie sheet and let stand until cool enough to handle. Then pull taffy until mixture is white and begins to hold shape. Mold into a rope about 3/4 inch thick. Cut into 1 inch pieces with scissors. Wrap each piece in wax paper or plastic.

(To prevent hands from becoming sticky while pulling taffy, grease hands with butter.) This recipe makes about a pound of candy.

Cranberry-Orange Sherbet

1 envelope unflavored GELATIN
½ cup COLD WATER
1 lb. raw CRANBERRIES
2 cups SUGAR
½ cup fresh ORANGE JUICE
2 cups WATER
1½ cups LIGHT CREAM

Soften gelatin in 1/2 cup cold water. Combine cranberries, sugar and orange juice with two cups water in a saucepan. Bring to a boil and cook until cranberries pop.

Add gelatin mixture and stir until completely dissolved. Remove from heat and cool.

Pour cooked mixture (a little at a time) into a blender and blend until smooth. Add cream and continue blending. Pour mixture into refrigerator tray and freeze until slushy. Remove from tray and beat mixture at high speed until thick and creamy. Put back into refrigerator tray and freeze until firm. (Makes about 2 quarts.)

Gold 'n Yellow Sherbet

6 fresh LEMONS (medium size)
2 large fresh ORANGES
3 tablespoons CORN STARCH
Dash of SALT
3 cups WATER
3 cups CONDENSED MILK

Juice the lemons and oranges. Strain the juice. In top of double boiler, combine corn starch, salt and water. Mix well. Add fruit juices and condensed milk. Cook, stirring constantly, until mixture thickens slightly. Remove from heat and chill in refrigerator two hours.

Pour cooled mixture into ice cream churn and freeze according to ice cream maker directions. (Makes 1/2 gallon sherbet.)

Sugarless Orange Sherbet

6½ cups fresh ORANGE JUICE
½ cup fresh LEMON JUICE
10 SACCHARIN TABLETS

Combine all ingredients and mix well. Pour into ice cream churn and freeze according to ice cream maker directions. (Makes 1/2 gallon sherbet.)

Winter Sherbet

2½ cups SUGAR
2 cups WATER
2½ cups fresh TANGERINE JUICE
4 drops ORANGE FOOD COLOR
3 EGG WHITES (beaten stiff)

Combine sugar and water in a saucepan and bring to a boil, stirring until sugar is dissolved. Boil for five minutes. Cool.

Add juice and food color and mix well. Pour mixture into freezing trays and freeze until mushy.

With beater, beat hard. Fold in egg whites and beat lightly. Return to freezing trays. Freeze until firm.

Old-Fashioned Lemon Sherbet

1 envelope unflavored
  GELATIN
2¼ cups cold WATER
1½ cups SUGAR
½ cup fresh
  LEMON JUICE

1/8 teaspoon SALT
1 teaspoon VANILLA
  EXTRACT
1½ teaspoons fresh
  LEMON PEEL (grated)
1 EGG WHITE

Soften gelatin in 1/4 cup of the cold water. Combine sugar with remaining two cups water and bring to a boiling point. Boil three minutes. Remove from heat and stir in gelatin mixture.

Add lemon juice, salt, vanilla extract and grated peel. Pour into freezing tray and freeze until almost firm.

Remove mixture from freezing tray into a large bowl. Add egg white and beat until fluffy and smooth. Return to freezing tray and freeze until firm.

Show-Off Orange Ice Cream

4 cups fresh ORANGE JUICE
2/3 cup SUGAR
2 cups HEAVY CREAM
1½ cups EVAPORATED MILK
1/8 teaspoon SALT

Combine all ingredients and mix until sugar is dissolved. Pour mixture into an ice cream churn and freeze according to ice cream maker directions. (Makes 1/2 gallon ice cream.)

Creamy Orange Sherbet

1½ cups WATER
1 cup SUGAR
1/8 teaspoon SALT
2 cups fresh ground ORANGE (about
    2 to 3 oranges)
2 teaspoons fresh LEMON JUICE
2½ cups MILK

Combine water, sugar, and salt in a saucepan. Bring to a boil, stirring until sugar is dissolved. Boil 10 minutes. Remove from heat and cool.

While mixture is cooling, quarter oranges and put through food grinder (using both peel and pulp). Add lemon juice.

After the water and sugar mixture has cooled, combine with ground citrus. Add milk and stir until well mixed. Pour mixture into ice cream churn and feeze according to ice cream maker directions. (Makes 1/2 gallon sherbet.)

Grapefruit Sherbet

1 tablespoon
    unflavored GELATIN
¼ cup cold WATER
2 cups SUGAR
1 cup WATER
5 cups fresh
    GRAPEFRUIT JUICE
1/8 teaspoon SALT

Soften gelatin in 1/4 cup cold water and set aside. Combine sugar and one cup water in saucepan and bring to a full boil, stirring until sugar is dissolved. Boil for two minutes. Remove from heat.

Add gelatin mixture, blending well. Add grapefruit juice and salt. Chill. Pour chilled mix into ice cream churn and freeze. (Makes 1/2 gallon sherbet.)

Kumquat Ice Cream Sauce

WATER for boiling
½ to ¾ cup fresh
    KUMQUATS
    (finely chopped)
1 cup HONEY
1 cup ORANGE JUICE
1/8 teaspoon SALT
1 tablespoon BUTTER

Bring water to boil in double boiler. Remove from heat. In top of double boiler, mix honey and orange juice until well blended. Add remaining ingredients, and (without cooking) let mixture stand over hot water for about 30 minutes to blend the flavors. Pour into clean container and store covered in refrigerator. Serve over ice cream.

BEVERAGES

Breakfast Drink

1 medium EGG
1 tablespoon HONEY
8 oz. GRAPEFRUIT JUICE

Beat egg with rotary or electric beater. Add grapefruit juice and honey. Beat again until thoroughly blended. (Serves 2)

Sunshine Shake

1 can (6-oz.) frozen concentrated
    ORANGE JUICE, undiluted
1 cup MILK
2 cups vanilla ICE CREAM

Place all ingredients in a two-quart jar. Cover jar tightly. Shake well. (Serves 8)

Cafe Brulot

1 ORANGE
4 sticks CINNAMON
2 CLOVES (whole)
6 cubes SUGAR
½ cup warm BRANDY
4 cups hot COFFEE (double-strength)

Cut rind from orange in thin strips and place in a chafing dish with cinnamon, cloves and sugar cubes. Pour in warm brandy and light with a match. Stir until flames die down and sugar is melted. Add hot coffee and serve in demi-tasse cups. (Makes one quart)

Breakfast Bracer

2 EGG YOLKS (beaten)
Juice of 4 ORANGES
2 teaspoons HONEY
Pinch of SALT

Beat all ingredients together and drink immediately. (Makes 2 drinks)

65

Lemonade

1 cup SUGAR
1 cup LEMON JUICE
6½ cups COLD WATER

Combine sugar and lemon juice and stir until sugar is dissolved. Add water, stir, and refrigerate. (Makes two quarts.)

Spicy Lemonade

4 cups WATER
1 cup SUGAR
10 Whole CLOVES
10 Whole ALLSPICE
2 CINNAMON STICKS
2½ cups ICE (crushed)
1 cup LEMON JUICE

Combine water, sugar and spices in saucepan and bring mixture to a boil. Simmer, uncovered, for five minutes. Remove spices. Pour into two-quart pitcher and chill. Add ice and lemon juice to pitcher and serve. (Makes 1½ quarts.)

Hot Buttered Lemonade

1 teaspoon LEMON PEEL (grated)
½ cup LEMON JUICE (fresh)
3 cups WATER
½ cup SUGAR
¼ cup light RUM
1 tablespoon BUTTER

Combine all ingredients in a saucepan and heat slowly. Pour into four serving cups.

Fresh Lemon Lemonade

1 cup SUGAR
1 cup LEMON JUICE (fresh)
2½ cups COLD WATER
1 LEMON

Slice unpeeled lemon. Dissolve sugar in lemon juice, add water and lemon slices. Pour into pitcher, cover, and chill in refrigerator. (Makes 4 cups)

Hot Lemonade Tea Punch

4 quarts WATER
1 teaspoon CLOVES (whole)
4 sticks CINNAMON
1/3 cup Loose TEA (or 15 bags)
1¼ cups SUGAR
1 cup ORANGE JUICE
1 cup PINEAPPLE JUICE
¾ cup LEMON JUICE (fresh)

Add cloves and cinnamon to water and bring to a full rolling boil. Remove from heat. Add tea immediately! Brew five minutes, stir and strain. Add sugar and stir til dissolved. Add fruit juices.

To reheat (before serving), place over low heat. DO NOT SIMMER or BOIL. Garnish with lemon slices. (Serves 25)

Spiced Tea

24 cups BOILING WATER
1 teaspoon CINNAMON
1 teaspoon CLOVES
JUICE of 3 LEMONS
JUICE of 6 ORANGES
1 to 2 cups SUGAR
5 teaspoons TEA

Bring water to a rolling boil. Put cinnamon and cloves into cloth bag and tie. Put tea into another bag and tie. Steep both bags in boiling water for five mintues. Remove bags and add balance of ingredients, stirring to dissolve sugar. Serve immediately while hot.

Honey Punch

1 cup ORANGE JUICE
½ cup LEMON JUICE
½ cup GRAPEFRUIT JUICE
2 cups WATER
5 tablespoons HONEY

Combine all ingredients and blend thoroughly. Chill and serve. (Makes 4 drinks)

Champagne Tea Punch

1 quart WATER
¼ cup LOOSE TEA
¼ cup RUM
¼ cup BRANDY
JUICE of 2 LEMONS
2 cups SUGAR
1 cup WATER
1 quart SODA WATER (chilled)
1 quart CHAMPAGNE (chilled)

Bring one quart of water to a rolling boil and remove from heat. Add tea immediately! Brew for five minutes. Stir and strain. Add rum, brandy and lemon juice. Cool at room temperature.

Boil sugar and one cup water to make syrup. Cool and chill thoroughly. At serving time, pour tea mixture, chilled syrup, soda water and champagne into punch bowl. Place ice cubes in champagne glasses and fill with punch. (Serves 25)

Happy New Year Punch

2 quarts ORANGE JUICE
1 cup GRAND MARNIER
1 quart STRAWBERRY SODA
ICE

Combine orange juice and Grand Marnier in large punch bowl. Slowly add strawberry soda. Add a block of ice or ice cubes to punch before serving. Garnish with orange slices and maraschino cherries. (Serves 24)

Citrus Mint Cocktail

1 cup ORANGE JUICE
1 cup GRAPEFRUIT JUICE
⅛ teaspoon PEPPERMINT EXTRACT
Crushed ICE

Combine juices with peppermint extract. Pour into small glasses over crushed ice. Garnish with fresh mint. (Makes four 4-oz. servings.)

Sangria Punch

1 bottle (fifth)
  BURGUNDY WINE
2 cups fresh
  ORANGE JUICE
1 ORANGE (sliced)

1 LEMON (sliced)
1 LIME (sliced)
2 to 4 cups GINGER ALE
  (chilled)

Combine wine, orange juice and fruit slices in large pitcher. Chill. Before serving, add ginger ale, as desired.

Verde Punch

3 quarts LIME JUICE
1 quart LIME SHERBET
1 (28-oz.) bottle LEMON-LIME SODA

Mix all ingredients in large punch bowl. Add a dash of brandy, if desired. Float slices of lemon and oranges for colorful effect.

Sunset Punch

1 qt. WATER
1 pint SUGAR
Grated PEEL from ½ LEMON
JUICE of 2 fresh LEMONS
1 pint fresh ORANGE JUICE

Combine water and sugar in saucepan, bring to a boil, and boil 10 minutes. Steep grated lemon peel in sugar syrup, strain, and add lemon juice. Cool and add orange juice. Chill and Serve.

Hot Spiced Punch

1 cup SUGAR
1 cup BROWN SUGAR
1 quart TEA (medium strenth)
4 sticks CINNAMON
6 CLOVES (whole)
2 quarts ORANGE JUICE
2 cups LEMON JUICE
ORANGE SLICES (thin)

Combine sugars, tea, cinnamon sticks and cloves and boil five minutes. Heat orange juice and lemon juice separately to boiling point. Combine with first mixture and pour into punch bowl. Float fruit slices on top. (Serves 30)

Holiday Punch

PEEL of 1 LEMON (thin strips)
1 cup SUGAR
1 cup WATER
2 teaspoons Crystallized GINGER
  (chopped fine)
4 CLOVES (whole)
2 CINNAMON STICKS
4 cups COLD WATER
1 cup LEMON JUICE (fresh)

Combine lemon peel, sugar, one cup water, ginger, cloves and cinnamon in a saucepan. Bring to a boil and stir to dissolve the sugar. Simmer five minutes and cool. Strain the peel and spices and discard. In a large pitcher, combine the sugar mixture, four cups cold water and lemon juice. To serve, pour over ice cubes. (Makes 6 cups)

Party Punch

5 cups ORANGE JUICE
2½ cups MARASCHINO CHERRY
  SYRUP
5 cups LEMON SODA

Combine orange juice and cherry syrup in large punch bowls. Slowly add lemon soda. Add a block of ice or ice cubes to punch before serving. Garnish with orange slices and cherries. (Serves 24)

Instant Fresh Lemonade Base

1 tablespoon fresh LEMON PEEL
  (grated)
1½ cups SUGAR
½ cup boiling WATER
1½ cups fresh LEMON JUICE

Combine lemon peel, sugar, and boiling water in a jar. Cover and shake until sugar dissolves. Add lemon juice. Store in refrigerator.

When serving, add 1/4 cup base syrup to one cup water in a tall glass with ice cubes.

Icy Orange Shrub

1 pint LEMON SHERBET
¼ cup APRICOT PRESERVES
1 can (6 oz.) Frozen ORANGE JUICE
   Concentrate (thawed, undiluted)
Crushed ICE

Soften sherbet and blend with preserves. Stir in orange concentrate. Fill 8 large glasses with crushed ice. Add orange mixture and stir. (To be drunk slowly, as ice melts.)

Citrus Cooler

4 cups ORANGE JUICE (divided)
1 cup FRESH MINT (snipped)
1 cup SUGAR
½ cup LIME JUICE
2 bottles (7-oz. each) SPARKLING
   WATER (chilled)

Heat two cups of orange juice just to a boil. Combine mint and sugar and mash with a fork. Pour hot orange juice over mint and cool. Strain and add remaining orange juice and lime juice. Chill. Immediately before serving, add sparkling water. Pour into chilled glasses with frosted rims. (Makes 8 drinks.) (To frost glasses, dip rim into orange juice and then into granulated sugar. Chill glasses.)

Citrus Punch Bowl

2 pints Raspberry SHERBET
1 cup LEMON JUICE (fresh)
1 cup ORANGE JUICE (fresh)
¾ cup SUGAR
2 bottles (28-oz. each) GINGER ALE
1 bottle (32-oz.) CRANBERRY JUICE

Soften one pint of sherbet and combine with lemon juice, orange juice and sugar in a punchbowl. Stir to dissolve the sugar. Add chilled ginger ale and cranberry juice.

With an ice cream scoop, float the remaining sherbet on top of the punch. (Makes about 15 cups)

Citrus Half and Half

1 cup ORANGE JUICE
8 tablespoons LEMON JUICE
8 tablespoons SUGAR
Ice CUBES

Combine orange juice, lemon juice, sugar and stir until sugar is dissolved. Pour over ice cubes in glass and add cold water to fill. (Serves 4)

Pick-A-Flavor Syrup

1 cup JUICE (orange, lemon or lime)
2 cups SUGAR

Put juice in small saucepan and stir in sugar. Heat over medium heat, stirring constantly until sugar is dissolved. Bring mixture to a full rolling boil. Remove from heat and cool to room temperature. Pour into covered jar and refrigerate.

This syrup will keep from two to three months in a covered refrigerator container.

Pick-A-Flavor Ice Cream Soda

2 tablespoons SYRUP (orange, lemon
   or lime)
CARBONATED WATER (chilled)
VANILLA ICE CREAM
Grated ORANGE or LEMON RIND

Put syrup in tall glass. Add small amount of carbonated water and stir. Add ice cream and fill glass with more carbonated water. Sprinkle with citrus rind.

Desert Quencher

4 cups GRAPE JUICE
1 cup fresh ORANGE JUICE
¼ cup LIME JUICE
1 cup cold WATER

Combine ingredients and sweeten to taste. Mix thoroughly and pour over crushed ice in tall glasses.

Orange Breakfast Drink

6 tablespoons Frozen ORANGE
    JUICE Concentrate (thawed,
    undiluted)
¾ cup COLD WATER
1 cup MILK
½ BANANA
1 cup CORN FLAKES
1 EGG
1 tablespoon SUGAR

    Combine all ingredients in blender container. Cover and process at high speed until smooth. (Makes 2 drinks)

Orange-Carrot Drink

1½ cups ORANGE JUICE
1½ cups MILK
2 CARROTS
¼ cup HONEY

    Clean carrots and cut in small pieces. Combine with other ingredients in blender. Cover and process at high speed until carrot is liquefied. Serve immediately. (Makes 1 quart)

Orange Shake

1 can (6 oz.) Frozen ORANGE JUICE
    Concentrate (thawed, undiluted)
1½ cups VANILLA ICE CREAM
2¼ cups MILK
4 scoops VANILLA ICE CREAM

    Combine juice concentrate with 1½ cups ice cream and milk in an electric blender. Cover and process at high speed until smooth. Pour into four glasses, top with scoops of ice cream. (Makes 4 drinks.)

★ ★ ★

    Hot lemonade can be made speedily by adding a cup of boiling water to the juice of two lemons.

★ ★ ★

    To make a lemon fizz drink, substitute carbonated water for water in your favorite lemonade recipe.

BREADS

Sunny Morning Bread

1½ cups CORN FLAKES
2 cups FLOUR
3 teaspoons
　BAKING POWDER
½ teaspoon SALT
½ cup BUTTER (softened)

½ cup SUGAR
2 EGGS
1 tablespoon ORANGE
　RIND (grated)
1 cup ORANGE JUICE
½ cup RAISINS (seedless)
½ cup NUTS (chopped fine)

Measure corn flakes and crush to fill 3/4 cup. Set aside. Sift together flour, baking powder and salt. Set aside.

Cream butter and sugar in mixing bowl until light and fluffy. Add eggs and orange rind and beat well. Stir in orange juice, mixing until well blended. Add flour mixture, stirring only until combined.

Stir in corn flakes, nuts and raisins. Spread in well-greased 9x5x3 pan. Bake in 350 F oven about one hour. Cool in pan 10 minutes before removing. Set bread on wire rack to cool completely before slicing.

(To double the recipe, increase ingredients proportionately and bake in greased and floured 10-inch tube pan. Bake in 350 F oven about 1½ hours.)

Orange Nut Bread

2/3 cup SUGAR
¼ cup SHORTENING
2 EGGS
2 cups FLOUR
3 teaspoons BAKING POWDER
½ teaspoon SALT
1 cup ORANGE JUICE
½ teaspoon VANILLA
2/3 cup NUTS (chopped)

Beat sugar, shortening and eggs until creamy. Mix flour, baking powder, and salt thoroughly. Stir into egg mixture alternately with liquid and vanilla. Stir nuts into last portion of flour mixture before blending it into batter.

Pour into greased 9x5x3 loaf pan. Bake in 350 F oven 50 to 60 minutes. Remove from pan and cool on rack.

Tangy Orange Bread

½ cup ORANGE RIND
  (3 oranges)
½ cup SUGAR
¼ cup WATER
1 tablespoon BUTTER
1 cup ORANGE JUICE
1 EGG (well beaten)

2½ cups FLOUR (sifted)
3 teaspoons BAKING
  POWDER
¼ teaspoon BAKING
  SODA
½ teaspoon SALT

Wash oranges, dry, and remove the thin outer rind with a sharp knife. Cut rind into very thin slivers with scissors.

Combine sugar and water in saucepan, add rind, and stir constantly over low heat until sugar is melted. Simmer about five minutes. (Peel and syrup should measure 2/3 cup.)

Add butter, stir until melted, and add orange juice and egg. Sift flour, baking powder, soda and salt into separate bowl. Add orange mixture and stir just enough to moisten. (Batter should be lumpy.) Pour into greased 9x5x3 loaf pan. Bake in 325 F oven for one hour and 15 minutes. Turn out on rack to cool.

Nutty Orange Loaf

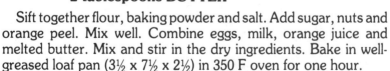

3 cups FLOUR (sifted)
6 teaspoons BAKING POWDER
1 teaspoon SALT
1 cup SUGAR
1 cup NUTS (ground)
½ cup ORANGE PEEL
2 EGGS (well beaten)
1 cup MILK
¼ cup ORANGE JUICE
2 tablespoons BUTTER

Sift together flour, baking powder and salt. Add sugar, nuts and orange peel. Mix well. Combine eggs, milk, orange juice and melted butter. Mix and stir in the dry ingredients. Bake in well-greased loaf pan (3½ x 7½ x 2½) in 350 F oven for one hour.

Orange Peel

Quarter two oranges. Remove peel. Cover peel with boiling water and simmer until tender. Scrape white membrane from inside peel and discard. Cut peel into strips, drain, and dry thoroughly.

Orange-Apricot Bread

½ cup DRIED APRICOTS
1 ORANGE
½ cup RAISINS
½ cup NUTS (chopped)
2 tablespoons BUTTER
1 1/3 cup SUGAR

1 teaspoon VANILLA
1 EGG
2 cups FLOUR (sifted)
2 teaspoons BAKING POWDER
¼ teaspoon SODA
¼ teaspoon SALT

Soak apricots in enough cold water to cover for 1/2 hour. Squeeze juice from orange into a meauring cup and add enough boiling water to make 1 cup. Put orange skins, apricots (drain first), and raisins through a food chopper. Cream butter and sugar, add vanilla, egg, and fruit mixture and beat smooth. Add dry ingredients alternately with orange juice and water, blending after each addition. Bake at 350 F one hour in greased, floured 9x5 pan.

Orange Coconut Loaf

3 cups all-purpose FLOUR
3 teaspoons BAKING POWDER
½ teaspoon SALT
1/3 cup Shredded COCONUT
1 EGG
1 cup MILK
1¼ cups ORANGE SYRUP

Measure and sift together flour, baking powder and salt. Add coconut. Beat egg and add milk to egg. Add orange syrup and egg mixture to dry ingredients. Stir only long enough to blend. Pour into greased 9x3x2 pan and bake in 350 F oven for one hour. (Bread tastes better one day after baking.)

Orange Syrup

Rind of 3 ORANGES
1 cup WATER
1 teaspoon SALT
1 cup SUGAR
¾ cup WATER

Cook rind in one cup of water and salt until rind is tender. Drain rind and cut up fine. Cook again with one cup sugar and 3/4 cup water until rind becomes transparent. Cool before using.

Orange Bread

5 tablespoons BUTTER
½ cup SUGAR
1 EGG
3 tablespoons ORANGE
  RIND
½ cup WATER

½ cup ORANGE JUICE
2 cups FLOUR
4 teaspoons BAKING
  POWDER
½ teaspoon SALT

Cream butter and add sugar gradually, creaming while adding. Add beaten egg and grated rind. Add water and orange juice alternately with flour, baking powder and salt which have been sifted together. Mix thoroughly, put in a greased pan (4½x8½) and let stand 20 minutes before baking. Bake at 350 F for 55 to 60 minutes.

Orange Waffles

3 cups FLOUR (unsifted)
6 teaspoons
  BAKING POWDER
1 teaspoon SALT
2 teaspoons SUGAR

6 EGGS
1 cup ORANGE JUICE
1½ cups LIGHT CREAM
½ cup BUTTER (melted)
2 teaspoons ORANGE
  RIND (grated)

In large bowl, mix together flour, baking powder, salt and sugar. In small bowl, beat egg yolks until light in color. To beaten yolks, stir in orange juice, cream, butter and orange rind. Add all at once to dry ingredients and stir to mix well. Beat egg whites until stiff peaks form and fold into mixture. Bake in waffle iron. Serve hot with Orange Currant Sauce. (Makes 6 waffles)

Orange Currant Sauce

1 tablespoon CORNSTARCH
½ cup ORANGE JUICE
½ cup CURRANT JELLY

Mix together cornstarch and orange juice. Add jelly. Cook over medium heat, stirring constantly, until jelly melts and sauce thickens and comes to a boil. Simmer over low heat for one minute. (Makes 1 cup)

77

Orange Date-Nut Bread

2 cups FLOUR (sifted)
2 teaspoons BAKING POWDER
½ teaspoon BAKING SODA
½ teaspoon SALT
½ cup NUTS (chopped)
¼ cup grated ORANGE PEEL
2/3 cup DATES (sliced, pitted)
1 EGG
1/3 cup ORANGE JUICE
2/3 cup WATER
½ cup SUGAR
1 teaspoon VANILLA EXTRACT
2 tablespoons BUTTER (melted)

Mix flour, baking powder, soda and salt and sift three times. Add nuts, orange peel and dates, and mix. Beat egg well and add remaining ingredients to beaten egg. Mix thoroughly. Add all at once to flour mixture and blend lightly (about 25 strokes). Pour batter into greased pan (10 x 3½ x 2¾) and let stand 20 minutes. Bake in preheated 325 F oven about one hour.

Orange Pancake Stacks

2 cups BISCUIT MIX
2 tablespoons ORANGE RIND (grated)
1 cup ORANGE JUICE
1/3 cup MILK
1 EGG
2 cups (1 lb.) COTTAGE CHEESE

Combine biscuit mix, orange rind and juice, milk and egg in bowl. Mix until moistened but still lumpy. Heat and lightly grease griddle. Pour 1/4 cup batter for each pancake, and turn once. Stack pancakes with 1/4 cup cottage cheese between each layer. Top with additional cheese and Orange Syrup.

Orange Syrup

1½ cups Light CORN SYRUP
1 can (6 oz.) Frozen ORANGE JUICE Concentrate (thawed, undiluted)

Mix corn syrup with concentrate until well blended. Pour over hot pancakes. (Sauce may be refrigerated.)

Banana Orange Bread

2 cups FLOUR (unsifted)
1 teaspoon
  BAKING SODA
¼ teaspoon SALT
½ cup BUTTER
1 cup SUGAR
2 EGGS

1½ cups BANANA
  (mashed)
¼ teaspoon ORANGE
  RIND (grated)
1½ tablespoons ORANGE
  JUICE
½ cup NUTS (chopped)

Combine flour, baking soda and salt and stir together thoroughly. In a large mixing bowl cream the butter and sugar. Beat in eggs. In a separate bowl, combine banana, orange rind and orange juice. Blend flour mixture (in 4 additions) alternately with banana mixture into creamed sugar. Stir in nuts and pour into greased 9x5x3 loaf pan.

Bake in 350 F oven for 1 hour, 10 minutes. Place pan on wire rack to cool for 10 minutes. Loosen sides of bread with metal spatula and turn out on wire rack. Turn right side up and cool.

Orange Crackling Bread

½ lb. SALT PORK (cubed)
2 tablespoons ONION
  (chopped fine)
1½ cups Yellow
  CORNMEAL
½ cup FLOUR (unsifted)

3 teaspoons BAKING
  POWDER
1½ teaspoons SALT
1 teaspoon SUGAR
2 EGGS
½ cup BUTTERMILK
1 cup ORANGE JUICE

In 9-inch ovenproof pan cook salt pork over low heat until very crisp. Remove and chop fine. Drain off all but one tablespoon fat. Add onion and cook until tender.

In large bowl, mix together cornmeal, flour, baking powder, salt and sugar. In small bowl, beat eggs with buttermilk and orange juice. Add egg mixture all at once to dry ingredients and stir just until mixed. Stir in salt pork and onion.

Heat pan, pour in batter and bake in 350 F oven for 30 minutes. Serve with hot butter. (Serves 8)

Lemon-Poppyseed Loaf

2 cups sifted FLOUR
1/3 cup SUGAR
3 teaspoons BAKING
POWDER
1 teaspoon SALT
2 tablespoons grated
LEMON PEEL

1 cup MILK
1 tablespoon
POPPYSEEDS
1 EGG (beaten)
¼ cup OIL

Sift flour, sugar, baking powder and salt in large bowl. Add lemon peel. In separate bowl, combine milk and poppyseeds. Stir egg and oil into milk. Add all at once to flour mixture and stir til dry ingredients are just moistened. Pour into greased 8x4 loaf pan. Bake in 350 F oven 1 1/4 hours (or til pick tests clean). Cool five minutes in pan on rack, then remove from pan and cool on rack.

Lemon Loaf

½ cup SHORTENING
2/3 cup SUGAR
2 EGGS
2¼ cups FLOUR
2 teaspoons BAKING POWDER
½ teaspoon SALT
1 cup MILK
2 teaspoons LEMON PEEL (grated)
½ cup NUTS

Cream shortening and sugar until light and fluffy. Add eggs separately, beating well after each addition. Sift together flour, baking powder and salt. Add to creamed mixture in three additions, alternating with milk. Beat until smooth. Stir in lemon peel and nuts. Pour into 9x5x3 pan and bake in 350 F oven for an hour (or until done). Let stand in pan 20 minutes before pouring glaze.

Lemony Glaze

½ cup POWDERED SUGAR (unsifted)
3 tablespoons LEMON JUICE (fresh)

Stir until sugar is dissolved and glaze is smooth consistency. Pour over hot cake before turning cake out onto rack.

Lemon Nut Bread

4 tablespoons BUTTER
1¼ cup SUGAR
2 EGGS
1½ teaspoons LEMON RIND (grated)
3¼ cups FLOUR (sifted)
3 teaspoons BAKING POWDER
½ teaspoon SODA
½ teaspoon SALT
2/3 cup MILK
4 tablespoons LEMON JUICE
¾ cup NUTS (coarse chopped)

Cream butter and sugar together. Blend in eggs and lemon rind. Stir in sifted dry ingredients alternately with milk and lemon juice. Fold in nuts. Spoon batter into lightly greased loaf pan (9x5x2). Bake in 350 F oven one hour. Remove from pan and cool.

Lemon Chocolate Loaf

2½ cups FLOUR
1 teaspoon BAKING POWDER
1 teaspoon SALT
1 cup SHORTENING
1½ cups SUGAR
4 EGGS (slightly beaten)
1 cup MILK
2 cups chopped NUTS
Grated rind of 2 LEMONS
2 (6-oz. pkgs.) semi-sweet CHOCOLATE BITS

Combine flour, baking powder, and salt. In another bowl combine shortening and sugar, beating til light and creamy. Add eggs, beating lightly. Add flour mixture and milk alternately, blending well after each addition. Stir in nuts, lemon rind, and chocolate bits. Pour into two greased loaf pans; bake in 350 F oven for 50 to 60 minutes. Cool and remove from pans.

Orange Cinnamon Toast

6 slices BREAD (white)
2 tablespoons frozen ORANGE JUICE concentrate (undiluted)
½ cup SUGAR
2 teaspoons CINNAMON
2 tablespoons BUTTER (melted)

Place bread on broiler pan. Preheat broiler to 375 F. Toast bread lightly on one side. Combine orange juice concentrate, sugar, cinnamon and butter. Turn bread and brush with orange mixture. Toast 4 minutes or until lightly browned.

CAKES

Sunny Orange Cake

1 ORANGE (medium)
1 cup RAISINS
½ cup NUTS
½ cup SHORTENING
1 cup SUGAR
2 EGGS (separated)
¼ teaspoon SALT

1¾ cups all-purpose
  FLOUR
½ teaspoon
  BAKING SODA
1 teaspoon
  BAKING POWDER
2/3 cup MILK
2/3 cup SUGAR

Juice the orange and set juice aside. Put orange rind, raisins and nuts through food chopper.

Cream shortening. Add sugar and cream thoroughly. Add egg yolks and salt, stir well.

Sift flour, soda, and baking powder together. Add alternately with milk to egg mixture.

Add ground fruit and nuts. Beat egg whites til stiff and fold in. Pour mixture into greased 8-inch tube pan.

Bake in 350 F oven about one hour. Mix 2/3 cup sugar with orange juice and pour over hot cake when it is taken from oven.

Orange Peanut Butter Cake

2 2/3 cups FLOUR (sifted)
1 cup SUGAR
2 teaspoons
  BAKING SODA
¾ teaspoon CINNAMON
¼ teaspoon SALT

2/3 cup BROWN SUGAR
  (packed)
1 cup PEANUT BUTTER
2 EGGS
1 1/3 cups ORANGE JUICE
1 ORANGE
1/3 cup BROWN SUGAR
  (packed)

Sift together first five ingredients into large bowl. Add 2/3 cup brown sugar, peanut butter, eggs and orange juice. Stir slightly to mix, then beat until batter is smooth (medium speed with mixer, 100 times by hand).

Grate one tablespoon orange peel. Then peel orange, cut into fine pieces and drain. Stir orange pieces and peel into batter. Pour batter into greased and floured 13x9x2 cake pan. Sprinkle 1/3 cup brown sugar evenly over top of batter. Bake at 325 F for 45 to 50 minutes. (Serves 12)

Orange Carrot Cake

1 cup soft BUTTER
2 cups SUGAR
1 teaspoon CINNAMON
½ teaspoon NUTMEG
1 tablespoon ORANGE
RIND (grated)
4 EGGS
1½ cups CARROTS (grated
or shredded)

2/3 cup WALNUTS
(chopped)
3 cups FLOUR (sifted)
3 teaspoons BAKING
POWDER
½ teaspoon SALT
1/3 cup ORANGE JUICE

In large bowl of electric mixer cream butter and sugar. Add cinnamon, nutmeg and orange rind. Beat in eggs, one at a time. Add carrots and nuts. Sift together flour, baking powder and salt and add alternately with the orange juice. Turn into a greased and floured 10-inch tube pan. Bake in 350 F oven for 60 minutes until cake tester inserted in cake comes out clean. Cool in pan 15 minutes, then turn out of pan and cool completely on wire rack. Cover top with Orange Glaze and decorate with orange slices. (Serves 10)

Orange Glaze

1½ cups CONFECTIONERS' SUGAR
(sifted)
1 tablespoon BUTTER (softened)
½ teaspoon ORANGE RIND (grated)
2 to 3 tablepoons ORANGE JUICE

In small bowl, beat confectioners' sugar with butter, orange rind, and enough orange juice to make a slightly-runny glaze.

Golden Orange Cake

2 cups FLOUR
3½ teaspoons
BAKING POWDER
¼ teaspoon SALT
½ cup BUTTER
1 cup SUGAR

4 EGG YOLKS
2/3 cup MILK
1 tablespoon
ORANGE JUICE
1 teaspoon ORANGE RIND
(grated)

Sift flour, baking powder and salt together. Cream butter thoroughly and add sugar gradually, creaming until sugar is dissolved. Add egg yolks and beat vigorously. Add flour mixture alternately with milk to creamed mixture. Add orange juice and orange rind. Beat until mixed thoroughly. Pour into two 8-inch greased and floured layer pans. Bake at 375 F for 30 minutes.

Orange Date Cake

1 cup BUTTER
2 cups SUGAR
4 EGGS
4 cups FLOUR (Cake)
1 teaspoon BAKING SODA
1 cup BUTTERMILK
2 tablespoons ORANGE RIND
  (grated)
1 lb. DATES (chopped, pitted)
1 cup NUTS (chopped)

Cream butter and sugar. Add eggs (one at a time), beating well after each addition. Sift flour and soda. Add to creamed mixture in three additions, alternating with buttermilk. Beat thoroughly until smooth. Add orange rind, dates and nuts and mix well. Bake in buttered Bundt pan in 350 F oven until it tests done (from 1 to 1½ hours). Remove from oven and cover with syrup.

While cake is baking, prepare syrup.

Orange Syrup

1 cup ORANGE JUICE (fresh)
2 cups SUGAR
1 tablespoon ORANGE RIND (grated)

Combine all ingredients and stir thoroughly until all sugar is dissolved. Pour gradually over hot cake in the Bundt pan. Allow cake to set in pan for ten minutes before removing. (Cake will stay moist for days.)

Orange Nut Cake

½ cup SHORTENING
1 cup SUGAR
3 EGGS (separated)
¼ teaspoon SALT
½ cup NUTS (chopped)
RIND of 1 LEMON (grated)
RIND of 1 ORANGE
  (grated)
1¾ cups FLOUR
3 teaspoons
  BAKING POWDER
½ cup ORANGE JUICE

Cream shortening and sugar. Add egg yolks and salt, and beat well. Add nuts and grated rind.

Sift flour and baking powder together and add alternately with orange juice.

Beat egg whites until stiff and fold in. Pour into two greased 8-inch layer pans and bake in 375 F oven 30 minutes. Frost as desired.

Velvet Orange Cake

1 cup SUGAR
½ cup SHORTENING
2 teaspoons ORANGE
  PEEL (grated)
1 EGG
2 cups FLOUR

1 teaspoon
  BAKING SODA
¼ teaspoon SALT
½ cup MILK
½ cup ORANGE JUICE
½ cup NUTS (chopped)
1 cup DATES (chopped)

Orange Glaze

½ cup ORANGE JUICE
1¼ cups POWDERED SUGAR

Cream shortening and sugar 'til light and fluffy. Add orange peel and egg and mix well. Combine flour, soda, and salt and add alternately to creamed mixture with milk and orange juice. Blend well. Add nuts and dates (lightly coated with teaspoonful of flour). Fold into mixture and pour into 9x11x2 glass baking pan. Bake 30 minutes in 350 F oven. Pour glaze over hot cake in baking pan. Cool and remove to cake dish.

Twelfth Night Cake

1 cup BUTTER
3 tablespoons frozen
  concentrate ORANGE
  JUICE (thawed,
  undiluted)
2 teaspoons ORANGE
  RIND (grated)
½ teaspoon VANILLA

¼ teaspoon SALT
4 whole EGGS (room
  temp.)
4 EGG YOLKS
(room temp.)
1 cup SUGAR
1½ cups FLOUR (sifted)
¼ cup CORNSTARCH
  (sifted)

Grease one 9-inch tube pan. In small saucepan, combine butter, orange concentrate, rind, vanilla, and salt. Stir over low heat until butter is melted. Remove from heat and cool to lukewarm. In large warm bowl, beat eggs, egg yolks and sugar until triple bulk. Gently sprinkle flour and cornstarch over eggs, add orange-butter mixture and very gently fold in until there is no trace of butter. Pour into pan. Bake in 350 F oven about 50 minutes (or until cake starts to come away from sides of pan). To serve, sprinkle top of cake with confectioners' sugar and garnish the sides with fresh orange slices if desired. (Serves 10)

Gold Dust Oatmeal Cookies

1 cup SHORTENING
2 cups SUGAR
2 EGGS
2 to 3 tablespoons fresh
  ORANGE JUICE
2 teaspoons ORANGE
  PEEL (grated)

2 cups FLOUR
4 teaspoons
  BAKING POWDER
1 teaspoon SALT
1 teaspoon NUTMEG
3 cups quick cooking
  ROLLED OATS

Cream shortening and sugar. Add eggs, orange juice and grated peel. Beat well. Add sifted dry ingredients and beat until smooth. Stir in rolled oats until well blended. Drop by teaspoon onto ungreased cookie sheet and bake in preheated 375 F oven for 12 to 15 minutes. (Makes about 60 cookies.)

Busy Bee Cookies

1/3 cup BUTTER
1/3 cup SHORTENING
1 cup HONEY
1 EGG
1 tablespoon ORANGE
  PEEL (grated)
½ cup COCONUT (flaked)

2¼ cups FLOUR
1 teaspoon
  BAKING POWDER
½ teaspoon BAKING SODA
1 teaspoon SALT
½ cup fresh
  ORANGE JUICE

Cream butter and shortening. Continue creaming while slowly adding honey in a fine stream. Add egg, orange peel and coconut. Add dry ingredients alternately with orange juice. Mix well.

Chill dough 30 minutes. Drop by teaspoon on a greased baking sheet. Bake in 375 F oven 15 to 18 minutes or until lightly browned. (Makes about 36 cookies.)

Orange - Nut Ginger Bars

1 pkg. GINGER BREAD MIX
¾ cup warm ORANGE JUICE
2 tablespoons ORANGE PEEL
  (grated)
1 cup NUTS (chopped)

Combine mix with orange juice. Add grated peel and chopped nuts. Pour into greased 9x9x1 3/4 pan. Bake in 350 F oven for 12 to 15 minutes. Cool. Frost with Orange Icing. Cut into bars.

Orange Filling

½ cup SUGAR
¼ cup FLOUR
½ cup WATER
1 tablespoon
   CORNSTARCH
½ ORANGE RIND (grated)
¼ cup ORANGE JUICE
½ tablespoon LEMON
   JUICE
1 EGG
1 tablespoon BUTTER

In top part of a double boiler mix sugar, flour, water and cornstarch. Add orange rind and cook over hot water until it thickens, stirring constantly. Let cook for 15 minutes more, stirring occasionally. Then add orange and lemon juice, beaten egg and butter. Stir vigorously and cook for 3 minutes. Remove top part of double boiler from the lower part and set aside to cool.

Lemon Filling

1 cup SUGAR
2½ tablespoons FLOUR
⅛ teaspoon SALT
¼ cup LEMON JUICE
RIND of 1 LEMON (grated)
2 EGGS
1 tablespoon BUTTER

Mix sugar, flour and salt thoroughly. Add lemon juice and rind, and cook in a double boiler for five minutes. Remove from heat. Beat eggs, and stir the sugar mixture slowly into them.

Return double boiler to heat and cook until thickened. Add the butter and stir slowly. Cool and use as filling for layer cake.

Orange Icing

2 tablespoons BUTTER
1 cup CONFECTIONERS SUGAR
2 tablespoons ORANGE JUICE
   (fresh)
RIND of 1 ORANGE (grated)

Cream the butter, and add sugar and orange juice gradually. Beat until soft and creamy. Spread at once on layer cake.

Orange Ring

1 cup BUTTER
1 cup SUGAR
3 EGGS (separated)
1 cup SOUR CREAM
2 tablespoons ORANGE RIND
   (grated)
1¾ cups FLOUR
1 teaspoon BAKING POWDER
1 teaspoon BAKING SODA

Cream butter and sugar until fluffy. Add egg yolks, sour cream and orange rind. Beat until fluffy. Sift together flour, baking powder and baking soda. Stir into creamed mixture. Beat egg whites until stiff (but not dry). Fold into batter. Pour into oiled and floured Bundt pan and bake at 325 F for one hour.

Let cake stand in pan for ten minutes. Then pour hot orange syrup over cooled cake.

Orange Syrup

½ cup SUGAR
Juice of 1 ORANGE
Juice of 1 LEMON
Dash of SALT

Combine ingredients in saucepan, bring to a boil and boil for three minutes. Pour immediately over cake.

Orange Drop Cookies

2 tablespoons
   ORANGE RIND (grated)
4 tablespoons BUTTER
1 cup SUGAR
2 EGGS (well beaten)

4 tablespoons
   ORANGE JUICE
2 cups FLOUR (sifted)
4 teaspoons
   BAKING POWDER
½ teaspoon SALT

Cream together the grated orange rind, butter and sugar. Add the eggs and orange juice and beat well. Combine flour, baking powder and salt and add to egg mixture. Drop the batter by spoonfuls onto greased baking sheet and bake in 350 F to 375 F oven for about 10 minutes. (Makes about 36 cookies)

Lemonade Cookies

1 cup BUTTER
1 cup SUGAR
2 EGGS
3 cups ALL-PURPOSE FLOUR
1 teaspoon BAKING SODA
1 can (6-oz.) FROZEN LEMONADE
   concentrate (thawed)

Cream butter and sugar thorougly. Add eggs, and beat till light and fluffy. Sift flour separately. Then sift together flour and soda. Add alternately to creamed mixture with 1/2 cup of the lemonade concentrate.

Scoop dough with teaspoon and drop two inches apart on ungreased cookie sheet. Bake in 400 F oven about eight minutes (or until lightly browned around edges). Brush hot cookies lightly with remaining lemonade concentrate. Sprinkle lightly with sugar and remove cookies to cooling rack. (Makes 4 dozen drop cookies)

Lemon Crumb Squares

1 can (15-oz.) CONDENSED MILK
½ cup LEMON JUICE
1 teaspoon LEMON RIND (grated)
2/3 cup BUTTER
1 cup BROWN SUGAR (firmly packed)
1 cup OATMEAL (uncooked)
1½ cups FLOUR (sifted)
1 teaspoon BAKING POWDER
½ teaspoon SALT

Blend milk, lemon juice and lemon rind together and set aside. Cream butter and blend in sugar. Add oatmeal and flour (sifted with baking powder and salt) to creamed mixture and mix until crumbly.

Spread half mixture in 8x12x2 buttered baking dish and pat down with fingers. Spread milk and lemon mixture in baking dish and cover with remaining crumbs. Bake in 350 F oven about 25 minutes (or until lightly browned at edges). Cool in pan at room temperature about 15 minutes. Cut into squares and chill in pan until firm.

Orange Sticky Buns

1/3 cup HONEY
6 tablespoons BUTTER
¼ cup frozen concentrated ORANGE
    JUICE, (thawed, undiluted)
¾ cup BROWN SUGAR (packed)
½ teaspoon CINNAMON
½ cup NUTS (chopped fine)
2 cans (10 oz. each) REFRIGERATED
    BISCUITS

Pour honey into 9-inch round cake pan and tilt to cover bottom. Melt butter in a small saucepan and add orange concentrate. In medium bowl mix brown sugar, cinnamon and nuts. Dip each biscuit into butter mixture and then into sugar mixture, shaking off excess. Stand biscuits upright in a circle around inside edge of cake pan. Bake in 375 F oven for 30 to 35 minutes. Cool in pan 15 minutes. Turn out onto plate and serve warm. (20 biscuits)

Orange Scones

2 2/3 cups FLOUR (unsifted)
1 teaspoon BAKING
    SODA
1 teaspoon BAKING
    POWDER
½ teaspoon SALT
2 tablespoons SUGAR
½ cup BUTTER

1 tablespoon ORANGE
    RIND (grated)
½ cup CURRANTS
3 tablespoons VINEGAR
¾ cup ORANGE JUICE
1 EGG (beaten)
MILK
SUGAR
BUTTER

Mix flour with baking soda, baking powder, salt and sugar. Cut in butter with two knives or pastry blender until mixture resembles coarse corn meal. Stir in orange rind and currants. Combine vinegar and orange juice. Make a well in center of flour mixture. Add liquid and egg all at once. Stir mixture with a fork until all dry ingredients are moistened. Turn onto a floured board. Knead gently 8 to 10 times, adding a little more flour if necessary. Roll into 12 x 6-inch rectangle. Cut into eight 3-inch squares. Cut each square in half diagonally, to make two triangles. Brush tops with milk and sprinkle with sugar. Place on greased baking sheets. Bake in 425 F oven for about 15 minutes (until golden brown). Serve with hot butter. (Makes 16 scones)

Orange-Orange Cake

½ cup BUTTER (or oleo)
1½ cups SUGAR
1 tablespoon ORANGE
  PEEL (grated)
2¼ cups FLOUR (sifted)
2 teaspoons
  BAKING POWDER
¼ teaspoon SODA
½ teaspoon SALT
¾ cup WATER
¼ cup fresh
  ORANGE JUICE
4 egg WHITES (beat stiff)

Beat butter (or oleo) with sugar until fluffy. Add orange peel. Sift flour, baking powder, soda and salt and add to butter mixture.

Combine water and orange juice and add alternately with dry ingredients, beating well. Fold in egg whites. Pour into two 8 inch round greased and floured cake pans. Bake in 375 F oven about 30 minutes (or until cake tests done). Cool five minutes and remove from pans. When cool, spread Orange Filling between layers and frost top and sides with Orange Buttercream Frosting.

Orange Filling

½ cup SUGAR
2 tablespoons CORN STARCH
1½ teaspoons ORANGE PEEL
  (grated)
¼ teaspoon SALT
¾ cup ORANGE JUICE
¼ cup WATER
2 EGG YOLKS
2 tablespoons BUTTER

Combine sugar, cornstarch, orange rind and salt in heavy saucepan. Gradually blend in orange juice, water and beaten egg yolks. Cook over medium heat, stirring constantly until mixture thickens. Cook three minutes. Remove from heat and stir in butter. Cool before spreading between layers.

Orange Buttercream Frosting

6 tablespoons BUTTER
4½ cups CONFECTIONERS SUGAR
  (sifted)
1 tablespoon ORANGE PEEL (grated)
Dash SALT
4 to 6 tablespoons ORANGE JUICE

In small deep bowl, cream butter, confectioners sugar, orange rind, salt and orange juice to spreading consistency. Beat until smooth and creamy.

91

Tangerine Cheesecake

Crust:
1 cup FLOUR (unsifted)
¼ cup SUGAR
1 tablespoon TANGERINE RIND (grated)
½ cup BUTTER
1 EGG YOLK
½ teaspoon VANILLA

Mix flour, sugar and grated tangerine rind in bowl. Add butter, egg yolk and vanilla. Cut in with pastry blender and then knead with fingers until smooth. Pat 1/3 of dough over bottom of 9-inch spring form pan. Bake in 400 F oven 5 minutes or until golden. Cool. Pat remaining dough evenly around sides to 1/2 inch from top.

Filling:
5 packages (8 oz. each) CREAM CHEESE (room temperature)
1¾ cups SUGAR
3 tablespoons FLOUR
1 tablespoon TANGERINE RIND (grated)
¼ teaspoon SALT
¼ teaspoon VANILLA
5 EGGS
2 EGG YOLKS
¼ cup TANGERINE JUICE

Place cream cheese in large bowl of electric mixer and beat at low speed until smooth and creamy. Mix together sugar, flour, grated tangerine rind and salt. Gradually beat into cream cheese, continuing to use low speed. Beat in eggs and egg yolks, one at a time. Blend in tangerine juice. Pour into prepared pan. Place aluminum foil under pan on oven rack and bake in 400 F oven 8 to 10 minutes, until crust browns lightly. Reduce heat to 225 F and bake 1 hour and 20 minutes longer. Cool slowly (do not put in cold place) and then refrigerate.

Tangerine Topping:
2/3 cup ground TANGERINES
1 cup SUGAR

To grind tangerines, cut into pieces and remove seeds. Put through medium blade of food chopper or grind in an electric blender. Measure and place in saucepan. Add sugar. Stir over moderate heat until sugar dissolves. Cook, stirring frequently, until mixture is thick like marmalade, 20 to 30 minutes. Cool and spoon over top of cheesecake before serving. (Serves 12)

Note: Oranges may be substituted for tangerines.

Lemon Bars

1 cup FLOUR
¼ cup BUTTER
¼ cup POWDERED SUGAR
2 EGGS
1 cup SUGAR
¼ teaspoon SALT
3 tablespoons LEMON JUICE
2 tablespoons FLOUR
½ teaspoon BAKING POWDER

Cream one cup flour with butter and powdered sugar. Press mixture into 8 or 9-inch square pan. Bake 20 minutes at 350 F and cool.

Mix eggs, sugar, salt and lemon juice. Add two tablespoons flour and baking powder, blending well. Pour mixture over cooled crust. Bake in 350 F oven for 25 to 30 minutes. Sprinkle with powdered sugar immediately on removing from oven. Cool thoroughly before cutting into bars.

Upside-Down Orange Biscuits

¼ cup BUTTER
½ cup ORANGE JUICE
½ cup SUGAR
2 teaspoons ORANGE
  RIND (grated)
2 cups FLOUR
½ teaspoon SALT
3 teaspoons BAKING
  POWDER
3 to 4 tablespoons
  SHORTENING
¾ cup MILK
¼ cup SUGAR
½ teaspoon CINNAMON

Combine butter, orange juice, 1/2 cup sugar and orange rind. Cook for two minutes. Pour into nine muffin tins. Sift flour, salt and baking powder. Cut in shortening. Add milk, and stir until dough follows fork around bowl. Knead for 1/2 minute and roll 1/4 inch thick. Sprinkle with remaining sugar and cinnamon. Roll as for jelly roll. Cut dough into 1-inch thick slices. Place cut side down, over orange mixture. Bake in 350 oven for 20 to 30 minutes.

★ ★ ★

To convert sweet milk to sour milk, put 1 1/2 tablespoons lemon juice in a standard measuring cup. Add fresh milk to the one-cup mark and let stand until soured. (Milk soured in this manner may be used like natural sour milk, or buttermilk, in any baking soda recipe.)

PIES

Lemon Chiffon Pie

Baked 9-inch PIE SHELL
1 envelope unflavored GELATIN
½ cup SUGAR
½ teaspoon SALT
4 EGG YOLKS
1/3 cup LEMON JUICE
2/3 cup WATER
1 teaspoon LEMON PEEL (grated)

In a saucepan, combine gelatin, sugar and salt. Beat egg yolks, lemon juice and water together, and add to gelatin mixture. Cook and stir over medium heat until mixture comes to a boil and gelatin is dissolved. Remove from heat and mix in lemon peel. Chill in refrigerator, stirring occasionally, til mixture is partially set.

4 EGG WHITES
½ cup SUGAR
½ cup CREAM (for whipping)

Beat whites until soft peaks form. Add sugar very gradually, beating until stiff peaks form. Fold in gelatin mixture. Whip cream and fold whipped cream into gelatin mixture. Pour into baked, cooled pie shell and chill until firm.

Lemon Coconut Pie

Unbaked 9-inch PIE SHELL
3 EGGS
1½ cups SUGAR
½ cup BUTTER (melted)
4 teaspoons LEMON JUICE
1 teaspoon VANILLA
1 1/3 cups FLAKED COCONUT

Beat eggs well and combine with all ingredients EXCEPT coconut. Stir in coconut and blend well. Pour into pie shell and bake in 350 F oven for 40 minutes. Cool thoroughly before serving.

No-Bake Lemon Pie

Graham Cracker PIE SHELL (8-inch)
1 EGG (well beaten)
½ cup fresh LEMON JUICE
3 teaspoons LEMON RIND (grated)
1 can sweetened CONDENSED MILK
1 teaspoon VANILLA
1 teaspoon LEMON RIND (grated)

Prepare crust, reserving 1/4 cup crumbs for topping. Chill well before adding filling.

Combine egg, juice, lemon rind, milk and vanilla. Stir until well blended. Pour into pie shell. Sprinkle reserved crumbs and one teaspoon lemon rind over pie top. Chill three hours in refrigerator before serving. (Keep remainder of pie refrigerated.)

Lemony Cheese Pie

2 cups GRAHAM CRACKER CRUMBS
   (about 14 double crackers)
½ cup BUTTER (melted)
1 cup (½ pint) WHIPPING CREAM
½ cup LEMON JUICE (fresh)
1 pkg. (8-oz.) CREAM CHEESE
1 can CONDENSED MILK
   (not evaporated)
1 envelope plain GELATIN
¼ cup COLD WATER
1 teaspoon VANILLA
1 cup (½ pint) SOUR CREAM

Combine graham cracker crumbs and butter. Line a 9-inch DEEP DISH pie plate with 3/4 of the crumb mixture. Stir lemon juice into cream and let stand 10 minutes.

Mash cream cheese thoroughly. Beat in condensed milk very gradually so mixture is smooth. Add gelatin to water. Let stand five minutes, then dissolve over hot water.

Whip lemon-cream mixture just until it begins to stiffen. Pour in cream cheese mixture and continue to beat until thoroughly blended. Stir in gelatin and vanilla.

Pour into pie crust and chill until firm (about 1½ to 2 hours). Top with sour cream and remaining crumbs.

95

Lemon Souffle Pie

Baked 10-inch PIE SHELL
1/3 cup LEMON JUICE
1 teaspoon LEMON PEEL (grated)
3 tablespoons HOT WATER
¼ teaspoon SALT
½ cup SUGAR
3 EGGS (separated)
¼ cup SUGAR

Combine lemon juice, lemon peel, hot water, salt, sugar, and egg yolks (well beaten) in top of double boiler, stirring occasionally, until thickened. Fold cooked mixture into egg whites, beaten with 1/4 cup sugar.

Pour into baked pie shell and bake in 325 F oven about 10-15 minutes, until lightly browned.

Lemony Tarts

5 Baked TART SHELLS
4 tablespoons CORNSTARCH
1 cup SUGAR
¼ teaspoon SALT
1 cup BOILING WATER
2 EGGS (separated)
6 tablespoons LEMON JUICE
RIND of 1 LEMON (grated)
1 tablespoon BUTTER

Mix cornstarch, sugar and salt. Add boiling water slowly, stirring to prevent lumps. Cook over low heat until thickened, stirring often. Add beaten egg yolks and remove at once from heat. Add lemon juice, rind and butter, stirring well. Pour into baked pastry shells. Cover with meringue and bake in 300 F oven 15 minutes.

Meringue

2 EGG WHITES
4 tablespoons SUGAR
½ teaspoon VANILLA

Beat egg whites until stiff (but not dry), adding sugar gradually. Add vanilla. Spread meringue over tarts.

Lemon Meringue Pie No. 1

Baked 9-inch PIE SHELL
1 cup SUGAR
1¼ cups WATER
1 tablespoon BUTTER
4 tablespoons
  CORNSTARCH

3 tablespoons
  COLD WATER
6 tablespoons LEMON
  JUICE
1 teaspoon LEMON RIND
  (grated)
3 EGG YOLKS
2 tablespoons MILK

Combine sugar, water and butter and heat until sugar dissolves, stirring slowly. Blend cornstarch and cold water and add to heated sugar mixture. Cook slowly until clear. Add lemon juice and grated rind and cook for two mintues. Combine egg yolks and milk and add to lemon mixture. Bring to boiling point and pour into pie shell. Cool, then cover with meringue.

Lemony Meringue

3 EGG WHITES
3 tablespoons SUGAR
1 teaspoon LEMON JUICE

Beat egg whites stiff but not dry. Add sugar and lemon juice. Spread over lemon filling and bake in 450 F oven 3 to 5 mintues.

Lemon Meringue Pie No. 2

6 tablespoons FLOUR
3 tablespoons CORNSTARCH
1 cup SUGAR
3 cups BOILING WATER
3 EGG YOLKS
RIND of 1 LEMON (grated)
½ cup LEMON JUICE
1 tablespoon BUTTER
¼ teaspoon SALT

Combine flour, cornstarch and sugar. Add boiling water, stirring constantly to prevent lumping. Cook slowly for fifteen minutes, stirring constantly. Beat egg yolks slightly. Slowly add part of hot liquid to yolks, beating constantly. Pour yolks into cornstarch mixture and cook over low flame until thickened. Remove from heat, and add remaining ingredients, mixing well. Pour into pie shell and top with meringue.

Sour Orange Meringue Pie

Baked 9-inch PIE SHELL
7 tablespoons CORNSTARCH
1¼ cups SUGAR
¼ teaspoon SALT
2 cups WATER
3 EGGS (separated)
1 tablespoon BUTTER
1 tablespoon SOUR ORANGE RIND
  (grated)
1/3 cup SOUR ORANGE JUICE

Mix cornstarch, sugar and salt in a saucepan. Stir in water slowly and mix until smooth. Cook on low until mixture is thick, stirring constantly. Continue cooking until mixture is very smooth. Stir a small amount of starch mixture into egg yolks and return to saucepan, stirring constantly. Remove from fire. Add butter, orange rind and juice to blend. Cool filling and pour into baked pie shell. Top with meringue and bake in 325 F oven for 20 minutes. Cool before serving.

Grapefruit Chiffon Pie

Baked 9-inch PIE SHELL
1 tablespoon GELATIN
¼ cup COLD WATER
4 EGGS (separated)
1 cup SUGAR
Dash of SALT
1 tablespoon GRAPEFRUIT RIND
  (grated)
½ cup GRAPEFRUIT pulp & juice
1 tablespoon LEMON JUICE

Soften gelatin in cold water. Beat egg yolks slightly. Combine gelatin, egg yolks and all other ingredients. Cook in top of double boiler, stirring constantly. Cool. As soon as mixture begins to thicken, fold in egg whites beaten with some sugar to form stiff peaks (but not dry). Turn into baked pie shell and chill thoroughly.

★ ★ ★

Add red or green coloring to syrup for candied citrus peel for a novelty effect.

Luscious Lime Pie

Unbaked 9-inch PIE SHELL
6 EGGS
2 cups SUGAR
5 or 6 LIMES (for 2/3 cup juice)
¼ cup BUTTER (melted)

Line pie pan with pastry and set aside. Beat eggs lightly in a mixing bowl, and add remaining ingredients. Beat until well blended. Pour into pasty shell. Bake at 325 F for 30 to 35 minutes, or until filling is set. Cool and chill before serving.

Two-Crust Grapefruit Pie

2 unbaked 8-inch PIE SHELLS
3 cups GRAPEFRUIT SECTIONS
½ cup BROWN SUGAR
3 tablespoons FLOUR
½ teaspoon CINNAMON
¼ teaspoon NUTMEG
2 tablespoons BUTTER

Line an 8-inch pie shell with pastry. Place grapefruit in pan in layers, sprinkling each layer with a mixture of the brown sugar, flour and spices. Dot with butter, top with pastry. Bake in hot oven (425 F) 30 mintues.

Lime Chiffon Pie

Baked 9 inch PIE SHELL
4 EGG YOLKS
1 (14-oz.) can sweetened
  CONDENSED MILK
½ cup fresh LIME JUICE
6 EGG WHITES
½ cup SUGAR
Pinch of
  CREAM OF TARTAR

Beat egg yolks until lemon colored. Stir in milk, lime juice and salt. Blend well. Beat egg whites until foamy. Add salt, cream of tartar and gradually add sugar. Beat until stiff. Set aside 1/4 of this mixture for topping.

Mix remaining 3/4 with egg yolk mixture. Fill pie shell and top with remaining meringue. Bake in 400 F oven for 8 to 10 minutes (or until top is lightly browned).

99

Lime Whip Pie

Baked 9 inch PIE SHELL
½ cup EVAPORATED MILK
1 envelope unflavored GELATIN
½ cup COLD WATER
4 EGGS (separated)
½ cup fresh LIME JUICE
1 cup SUGAR
½ teaspoon SALT
1 teaspoon LIME (grated)
Green FOOD COLORING

Chill milk in freezing tray until crystals form around edges. Sprinkle gelatin over cold water. Stir in egg yolks and chilled milk. Blend well. Add lime juice. Cook over low heat until gelatin dissolves and mixture thickens slightly.

Stir in 1/2 cup sugar, salt, grated rind and seven drops of food coloring. Chill thoroughly.

Beat egg whites. Add remaining 1/2 cup sugar. Fold gently into gelatin mixture. Turn into pie shell and garnish.

Lime Pie

Baked 9 inch PIE SHELL
1 cup SUGAR
3 tablespoons
  CORN STARCH
2 tablespoons FLOUR
Dash SALT

2 cups boiling WATER
3 EGG YOLKS
  (slightly beaten)
¼ cup LIME JUICE
Grated RIND of 1 LIME
1 tablespoon BUTTER

In top of double boiler, combine sugar, corn starch, flour and dash of salt. Stir in boiling water and cook over direct heat, stirring constantly until thickened. Gradually add egg yolks and cook over boiling water until quite thick. Remove from heat and add lime juice, grated peel and butter. Cool and pour into baked pie shell.

Lime Meringue

3 EGG WHITES
6 tablespoons SUGAR
1 tablespoon LIME JUICE

Beat egg whites until they begin to hold soft peaks, while adding sugar and lime juice. Spread over pie filling, making sure meringue touches the crust all around. Bake in 425 F oven for 5 to 6 minutes, or until golden tipped. Cool completely before serving.

Orange Pecan Pie

Unbaked 9 inch PIE SHELL
1 fresh ORANGE (medium size)
1½ cups BROWN SUGAR
1 cup light CORN SYRUP
3 tablespoons BUTTER
3 EGGS (well beaten)
1½ cups PECANS (broken)

Cut orange into quarters and remove any seeds. Put orange quarters, peel and pulp through a food chopper. Combine ground orange with sugar and corn syrup in saucepan. Bring to a full hard boil. Remove from heat. Cool slightly, stirring occasionally.

Add butter and cool a little more, still stirring (about five minutes). Blend in eggs and pecans, mixing thoroughly. Pour into unbaked pie shell and bake in 350 F oven approximately 40-45 minutes (or until set).

Orange Cream Pie

Baked 9 inch PIE SHELL
2 EGG YOLKS
¾ cup SUGAR
1 tablespoon FLOUR
1 tablespoon ORANGE PEEL (grated)
½ cup fresh ORANGE JUICE
1 cup HEAVY CREAM
1 teaspoon SUGAR

In top of double boiler, combine egg yolks, sugar, flour and orange peel. Mix well. Gradually add orange juice. Cook over boiling water, stirring occasionally until thickened. Chill thoroughly.

Beat cream until thick. Add one teaspoon of sugar and continue beating until stiff. Fold cream into orange mixture. Spoon into pastry shell. Chill until firm (at least four to six hours) before serving.

Coconut Piecrust

2 cups COCONUT (flaked)
¼ cup BUTTER

Combine coconut and softened butter in a 9 inch pie plate. Toast in 375 F oven 15 minutes, stirring occasionally until golden brown. Remove from oven and press mixture over bottom and sides of pan. Cool. This crust is delicious with any flavor creamed citrus filling.

101

Gold Rush Lemon Pie

Baked 9 inch PIE SHELL
1¼ cups SUGAR
¼ cup plus 2 heaping
  tablespoons FLOUR
1/8 teaspoon SALT
1 cup WATER
4 EGG YOLKS (beaten)

1 teaspoon fresh LEMON
  PEEL (grated)
½ cup fresh LEMON JUICE
1½ cups hot MILK
2 tablespoons BUTTER
4 EGG WHITES
8 tablespoons SUGAR
Dash SALT

Combine sugar, flour and salt in a heavy saucepan. Add water and stir til smooth. Blend in egg yolks, lemon peel and lemon juice. Add hot milk gradually and butter. Place over medium heat and bring to a boil, stirring constantly. Boil a full five minutes. Cool and pour into pastry shell.

Top with meringue made by beating egg whites til frothy, then adding sugar and salt gradually til peaks form. Place in 350 F oven til brown (about 5 minutes).

Orange Meringue Pie

1 baked 9-inch PIE SHELL
1½ cups ORANGE JUICE
1 cup SUGAR
RIND of 1 ORANGE (grated)
3 EGG YOLKS
1 tablespoon BUTTER
2 tablespoons CORNSTARCH
⅛ teaspoon SALT

Combine all ingredients in top of double boiler. Mix thoroughly, so that egg yolks are broken and blended. Set pot over double boiler and cook until thick. Chill completely before pouring into pie shell. Cover with meringue, making sure meringue touches the crust completely. Bake in 425 F oven until meringue browns lightly (about five minutes).

Orange Meringue

3 EGG WHITES
6 tablespoons SUGAR
1 tablespoon ORANGE JUICE

Beat egg whites until stiff. Gradually add the sugar and orange juice, beating thoroughly after each addition.

Orange Chiffon Pie

Baked 9 inch PIE SHELL
1 envelope
   unflavored GELATIN
¼ cup COLD WATER
4 EGGS (separated)
1 cup SUGAR
½ teaspoon SALT

½ cup fresh
   ORANGE JUICE
¼ cup fresh LEMON JUICE
2 teaspoons
   ORANGE PEEL (grated)
1 cup HEAVY CREAM

Soften gelatin in cold water. Combine in saucepan slightly beaten egg yolks, 1/2 cup sugar, orange and lemon juices, and grated peel. Cook over low heat, stirring constantly until slightly thickened. Remove from heat.

Add softened gelatin and stir until dissolved. Chill until mixture begins to thicken. Beat egg whites until foamy. Gradually add 1/2 cup sugar, beating until stiff peaks form.

Beat cream until thick. Fold gently, but thoroughly, into gelatin mixture. Then fold in egg whites. Spoon into pastry shell. Chill until firm (at least four hours) before slicing.

Citus Pastry

½ teaspoon SALT
1½ cups FLOUR
½ cup SHORTENING
About ¼ cup fresh ORANGE JUICE
1 teaspoon grated ORANGE PEEL

Mix salt and flour in large bowl. Cut in shortening with fork or pastry blender. (Work mixture with fingers until shortening is in pellets about the size of green peas. As shortening melts during the baking process, it leaves a space, making a flaky pie crust.)

Moisten the flour mixture with chilled orange juice, using only what is needed to make the dough hold together. Add grated peel and work in. Form into a ball, wrap in wax paper and chill about an hour.

Cut off enough dough to cover bottom and sides of pie pan. On a floured board, roll out dough in a circle about 1/8 to 1/4 inch thick. Line pie pan. Cut off excess and puncture bottom of crust with a fork.

If a top crust is required, repeat process, putting pastry over top of pie. Seal edges. Puncture or cut design in top crust. Bake according to recipe instructions.

MARMALADES

Preserved Whole Kumquats

2 cups fresh KUMQUATS **1 stick CINNAMON**
1 cup WATER **1 LEMON (thinly sliced)**
2 cups SUGAR

Wash and drain fruit. Cut a small "X" in each kumquat. Cover with water and bring to boil. Cook 5 minutes and drain. Combine water and sugar to make a syrup. Add cinnamon and lemons.

Drop kumquats into syrup. Bring to a boil and cook for 10 minutes. Cover and let stand overnight in refrigerator. Cook again, uncovered, for 10 minutes. Let stand to plump (at least overnight) in refrigerator. Return to heat, bring to a boil, and cook until fruit is clear and syrup thick, stirring frequently. Pour into sterile jars and seal.

Grapefruit Marmalade

2 medium GRAPEFRUIT
1/8 teaspoon BAKING SODA
2 cups HONEY
2 cups SUGAR
1 box powdered FRUIT PECTIN

Score grapefruit in quarters and remove peel. Scrape white part off with spoon and discard. With sharp scissors, slice peel very fine. Put peel in saucepan with water and soda. Bring to a boil and simmer, covered, for 15 minutes. Drain.

Add more water to cover, and bring to another boil, stirring occasionally until tender. Drain.

Chop pulp, removing any white membrane. Add to rind and measure three cups of mixture into large saucepan. Measure honey and sugar and set aside. Add pectin to fruit in saucepan and mix well.

Cook over high heat and stir until mixture comes to a full boil. Immediately stir in honey and sugar. Boil hard for one minute, stirring constantly. Remove from heat and skim off foam with metal spoon. Stir and skim seven minutes to cool slightly and prevent fruit from floating. Pour into hot sterilized 6-oz. jelly glasses. Seal at once with hot paraffin.
(Yield: about 8 glasses)

Citrus Marmalade

2 GRAPEFRUIT (Large)
4 ORANGES (Large)
2 LEMONS (Large)
WATER (to cover)
4 cups COLD WATER
10 cups SUGAR (about)
3 pieces GINGER ROOT
1 tablespoon VANILLA

Wash fruit, cut in thin strips, remove seeds. Cut each slice into 1/4 inch strips. Measure fruit, which should equal about seven cups grapefruit and almost six cups oranges.

Place fruit in deep pan, add water to cover, and bring to boiling point. Drain. Repeat process twice. Add 4 cups cold water, bring to a boil, reduce heat and simmer (uncovered), until fruit is tender (about 1½ hours).

Measure fruit. Add sugar (1 cup for each cup fruit) and ginger root. Cook over low heat, stirring frequently (about 2½ hours) until thickened. Add vanilla. Spoon marmalade into sterilized jars and seal at once.

Grapefruit Conserve

2 GRAPEFRUIT (large)
4 LEMONS
Boiling WATER
1½ cups SEEDLESS RAISINS (halved)
5 cups SUGAR
1 cup COCONUT (shredded)
½ teaspoon GINGER (ground)

Peel grapefruit and lemons and shred the rinds. Slice the pulp very thin. Add boiling water to barely cover. Add the raisins. Blend thoroughly and set aside in refrigerator overnight. Next day bring mixture to boiling point. Cook until tender, about 35 minutes, stirring frequently. Strain.

Boil down the juice rapidly to half its original bulk. Add strained fruit, sugar, coconut and ginger. Simmer five minutes, pour into sterile jars, and seal.

Lemon Marmalade

6 LEMONS (unpeeled)
SUGAR

Wash and slice lemons very thin. Cut slices into small pieces and measure fruit. Add three times as much water and boil until tender. Replace liquid boiled away with water. Allow about 3/4 cup sugar for each cup fruit juice.

Cook in two-cup batches for about 10 minutes each time, until thick drops fall from spoon. Pour into sterile jars and seal. (Makes eight 6-oz. jars.)

Kumquat Marmalade

3 cups KUMQUATS (finely chopped)
3 cups WATER
5 cups SUGAR
½ bottle CERTO

Put kumquats through food chopper on fine blade. Combine fruit with water and let stand overnight. Simmer for 1/2 hour. Add sugar and bring to rolling boil, stirring constantly for one minute. Remove from heat and add Certo. Stir and skim for six to seven minutes. Pour into sterilized jars and seal with paraffin.

Calamondin Marmalade

3 cups CALAMONDIN
1 cup PINEAPPLE (crushed)
1 cup WATER
2 tablespoons LEMON JUICE
1 pkg. PECTIN
6 cups SUGAR

Wash fruit and cut up into small pieces. Remove seeds. Cover with water and bring to a soft boil. Remove two cups of pulp and combine with pineapple, water and lemon juice. Add pectin and return mixture to pan. Bring to a hard boil over high heat, stirring frequently. Add sugar all at once. Bring to a full rolling boil and boil hard one minute, stirring constantly. Remove from heat, skim off foam. Continue stirring and skimming for five minutes until slightly cooled. Pour into six sterile jars and seal.

Lemon Honey

6 tablespoons BUTTER
1 cup SUGAR
3 EGG YOLKS
1 large LEMON (grated)

Cream butter and add sugar gradually. Heat creamed mixture in double boiler until butter melts. Beat egg yolks until thick, and add grated lemon rind. Pour into creamed mixture and stir until it thickens. Add lemon juice and continue stirring until the consistency of honey. Pour into sterilized jars and seal. Use as you would use honey.

Lemon Mincemeat

½ cup LEMON JUICE
1 cup RAISINS
3 cups APPLES (chopped fine)
½ cup NUTS (chopped)
¼ cup LEMON (or orange) MARMALADE
2 cups SUGAR
½ teaspoon SALT
2 teaspoons CINNAMON
1 teaspoon CLOVES
1 teaspoon GINGER

Scald, drain, and chop raisins. Combine with other ingredients and store in sterile jars. To use a pie filling add 1/4 cup melted butter for each pie. (Makes one quart mincemeat, or filling for two pies.)

Apple-Grapefruit Butter

1 cup APPLES (dried)
½ cup GRAPEFRUIT Segments
¼ ORANGE (thinly sliced)
1 1/3 cups SUGAR
3 cups Warm WATER

Wash apples and drain. Add water to cover and let· stand overnight. Simmer until soft. Add remaining ingredients. Simmer until thick. Pour into sterile jars and seal.

Old-Fashioned Orange Marmalade

6 ORANGES (peeled)
1 LEMON (unpeeled)
11 cups COLD WATER
7 cups SUGAR

Remove all white membranes from peeled oranges and slice thin. Slice unpeeled lemon. Cover oranges and lemon with water. Let stand in refrigerator for 24 hours. Boil for three hours, add sugar, and boil one more hour. Put into sterile jars and seal. (Makes about four pints)

3-Day Marmalade

5 SOUR ORANGES
1 GRAPEFRUIT
SUGAR

1st Day: Cut fruit in half and remove grapefruit seeds. With potato peeler cut pulp and rind in slices. Measure and add three times as much water as fruit. Let mixture stand overnight in refrigerator.

2nd Day: Boil mixture twenty minutes at hard boil and let stand in refrigerator.

3rd Day: Measure mixture and measure equal amount of sugar. Boil fruit mixture for 20 minutes and add sugar all at once. Stir. Boil 30 minutes more (or until mixture jells). Seal while hot.

Orange-Lemon Marmalade

3 ORANGES (unpeeled)
2 LEMONS (unpeeled)
5 cups SUGAR
5 cups WATER

Wash fruit and cut crosswise into thin slices, removing seeds. Put slices into deep pan, add water, and let stand in refrigerator 36 hours. Heat to boiling point, and boil (NOT simmer) two hours. Add sugar, and boil one hour more. Pour into sterile jars and seal.

Pickled Kumquats

2 cups HONEY
1 cup CIDER VINEGAR
3 fresh KUMQUATS
  (cut into thick slices)

3 inches STICK
  CINNAMON
12 whole CLOVES
1 cup WATER
Fresh FRUITS (pears,
  peaches, pineapple)

Combine honey, vinegar and kumquats in large pot. Heat to boiling and add spices. Continue boiling about five minutes. Have fruit ready (4 to 6 cups of quartered pears OR peach halves OR pineapple chunks). Add fruit to spiced mixture and cook until all fruit is tender. Pack fruit in hot jars, cover with boiling syrup and seal at once.

Old Timer's Lemon Curd

4 EGGS
1 lb. SUGAR
3 fresh LEMONS
3 oz. BUTTER (no subs.)

3 eggs
1 1/4 cups sugar
3 lemons
1/2 cup

Beat eggs. Combine with sugar, grated lemon peel, lemon juice, and butter in top of double boiler. Heat mixture and keep stirring until it thickens like honey. Bring almost to a boil (but do not allow to boil). Pour into small glasses and cover. Store in refrigerator. *for 1 week* (Excellent as spread or as small pastry filling.)

Sun Gem Marmalade

2 GRAPEFRUIT
2 LEMONS
2 ORANGES
2 cups WATER
¼ teaspoon SALT
SUGAR

Peel fruit. Cut peel into chunks and place in blender with water. Set blender on chop. Empty into a large kettle and bring to a full boil. Simmer for 20 minutes.

Place pulp from fruit into blender and whirl until pureed. Pour into measuring cup. Measure equal amount of sugar. Add pulp, sugar and salt to the cooked peel mixture. Bring to a boil. Turn heat down to simmer and simmer until thick and clear (about 20 minutes). Stir occasionally. Pour into hot sterilized jars and seal. (Yield: 2 pints)

Sour Orange Marmalade

6 SOUR ORANGES
2 quarts WATER
3 lbs. SUGAR
½ teaspoon SALT

Remove peel from two oranges. Slice peel very thin and cover with water. Boil until tender, adding more water as it boils away. (Change the water often if the flavor becomes too bitter.)

Peel remaining oranges (peel may be stored in freezer for later use). Boil pulp in two quarts water until very soft. Strain through a bag with pressure. Re-strain without pressure. Mix this juice with the drained peel, the sugar and the salt and boil until the jelly stage is reached. Let stand until slightly cool. Stir and pour into hot sterilized jars and seal with paraffin.

Sour Orange Preserves

4 SOUR ORANGES
1½ cups Sour Orange JUICE
1½ cups WATER
1½ cups SUGAR

Wash oranges. Peel skin (leaving as much of the thick white membrane as possible.) Cut in halves. Squeeze out juice, but handle carefully to avoid splitting halved orange shells. Cover with water in large pan and cook 10 minutes. Drain. Make a syrup of orange juice, water and sugar. Drop orange shell halves into syrup. Cook on low heat until rinds are transparent. Pack rinds in clean jars. Cover with hot syrup. Seal and place in jars in large pot of hot water. (The water should cover jars.) Simmer for 10 minutes to complete the seal and sterilize.

Yellow Tomato Preserve

3 fresh LEMONS
2 tablespoons POWDERED GINGER
7 lbs. ripe TOMATOES
5 lbs. SUGAR

Slice lemons very thin. Put ginger powder into small cloth bag and tie securely. Place all ingredients into large pot. Bring to hard rolling boil, stirring and mashing. Lower heat and boil slowly two to three hours. Remove from heat and cool slightly. Ladle into hot sterilized jars and seal. (Yield: about three quarts)

SAUCES

Simple Barbecue Sauce

2 tablespoons BUTTER (melted)
½ cup ONION (chopped)
2 tablespoons VINEGAR
2 tablespoons BROWN SUGAR
6 tablespoons LEMON JUICE
3 tablespoons Worcestershire SAUCE
1 bottle (14 oz.) KETCHUP
¼ teaspoon SALT
⅛ teaspoon BLACK PEPPER

Saute onion in butter until golden in color. Add remaining ingredients and stir well. Simmer on very low heat about 50 minutes, stirring often. Cool and pour into container. Store in refrigerator. (About 2 cups)

Lemon Barbecue Sauce

1 clove GARLIC
½ teaspoon SALT
¼ cup SALAD OIL
½ cup LEMON JUICE
2 tablespoons ONION (grated)
½ teaspoon BLACK PEPPER
1 teaspoon Worcestershire SAUCE

Mash garlic with salt in bowl. Stir in remainder of ingredients and chill for 24 hours. (About 3/4 cup)

Lemon Marinade for Steaks

1/3 cup LEMON JUICE
½ cup SALAD OIL
2 teaspoons ONION (chopped fine)
1 tablespoon WORCESTERSHIRE

Combine all ingredients and marinade steaks overnight.

Honey-Orange Sauce

1/3 cup HONEY
1 tablespoon CORNSTARCH
1 teaspoon ORANGE RIND (grated)
½ cup ORANGE JUICE
¼ cup WATER
2 tablespoons BUTTER

Combine honey, cornstarch and orange rind in a heavy saucepan. Stir in orange juice and water. Bring to a boil. Add butter and blend well. Cool slightly. Sauce will thicken as it cools. (Makes about one cup.) Can be spooned over desserts.

Lemon Medley Sauce

2 teaspoons LEMON RIND (grated)
½ cup LEMON JUICE (fresh)
2 cups SUGAR
¾ cup (1½ sticks) BUTTER
4 EGGS

Combine lemon rind and juice, sugar and butter. Cook over low heat until butter is melted and sugar is dissolved. Remove from heat. Beat eggs until thick and lemon colored. Stir and blend eggs thoroughly into lemon mixture. Return to heat. Cook, stirring constantly, until mixture coats a metal spoon. Cool and store in covered jar in refrigerator up to three months. (This sauce is ideal spooned over ice cream, as a filling for lemon tarts, and over puddings.) Makes 3 cups.

Lemon Shortcake Sauce

3 tablespoons CORNSTARCH
½ cup SUGAR
¼ teaspoon SALT
2 cups WATER
1 tablespoon LEMON PEEL (grated)
3 tablespoons LEMON JUICE
¼ cup BUTTER

Combine cornstarch, sugar and salt in saucepan. Add water gradually and cook over low heat, stirring until mixture comes to a boil and thickens. Remove from heat and add lemon peel, juice, and butter. Stir until butter melts completely. Cool and serve over shortcake. (Makes about 2 cups)

Lemon Hard Sauce

1/3 cup BUTTER (softened)
2¼ cups POWDERED SUGAR
1 EGG (separated)
3 tablespoons LEMON JUICE

Cream butter, sugar, egg yolk and lemon juice. Fold in egg white, stiffly beaten.

Lemon Sauce

1 tablespoon CORNSTARCH
½ cup SUGAR
1 teaspoon LEMON RIND (grated)
1 cup BOILING WATER
2 tablespoons LEMON JUICE
2 tablespoons BUTTER
Dash SALT

Combine cornstarch, sugar and grated rind in saucepan. Add boiling water gradually, stirring constantly. Boil five minutes and remove from fire. Add lemon juice, butter, and salt. Serve hot over puddings, cakes, etc. (Makes 4 servings)

Orange Sauce

Rind of 1 ORANGE (grated)
½ cup SUGAR
2 tablespoons CORNSTARCH
2/3 cup BOILING WATER
2 tablespoons BUTTER
1 EGG (well beaten)
2/3 cup ORANGE JUICE
1 teaspoon LEMON JUICE

Combine orange rind, sugar and cornstarch in pan. Mix well and add boiling water. Heat for 10 minutes, stirring constantly. Add butter and remove from heat. Pour over egg and return to pan. Cook two minutes, stirring constantly. Add juices, beat and cool. Serve cool over cakes, ice cream, etc. (Makes 4 servings)

Lemon Butter

¼ cup BUTTER
¼ teaspoon PAPRIKA
1 tablespoon LEMON JUICE

Cream butter and paprika together and add juice by drops, stirring constantly, until butter and juice are completely blended.

Piquant Lemon Butter

¼ cup BUTTER
¼ tablespoon RED PEPPER (chopped)
¼ tablespoon GREEN PEPPER (chopped)
¼ tablespoon PARSLEY (chopped)
1 teaspoon ONION (chopped)
¼ Clove GARLIC (chopped)
2 teaspoons LEMON JUICE

Cream butter thoroughly. Add other ingredients and mix well. (Ideal for broiled meats.)

Grapefruit Seafood Sauce

1 cup (½ pound) BUTTER
6 tablespoons frozen GRAPEFRUIT JUICE concentrate (thawed, undiluted)
1 teaspoon GRAPEFRUIT RIND (grated)
¼ cup PARSLEY (chopped)
2 tablespoons DILL (chopped)
2 tablespoons CHIVES (chopped)
¼ teaspoon SALT
Raw OYSTERS, CLAMS or cooked SHRIMP

Melt butter in saucepan. Add grapefruit concentrate, grapefruit rind, parsley, dill, chives and salt, and heat. Use as a dunk sauce for seafood. (Sauce makes 6 servings. Note: 2 teaspoons dried dill weed may substitute for fresh dill.)

Raisin Sauce

½ cup RAISINS
½ cup WATER
1/3 cup JELLY (any kind)
1/3 cup ORANGE JUICE
¼ cup BROWN SUGAR
1 tablespoon CORNSTARCH
Dash SALT
Dash ALLSPICE

Rinse raisins. Put raisins, water, jelly and orange juice into saucepan. Bring to a boil. Blend sugar with cornstarch, salt and allspice, and stir into orange mixture. Cook, stirring until clear. (Makes about 1 cup)

Honey Lime Glaze

1 cup HONEY
½ cup LIME JUICE
½ teaspoon SALT
½ teaspoon GINGER (ground)

Combine all ingredients. Mix well until blended. Brush over poultry during last 30 minutes of roasting. (Makes 1½ cups sauce)

Sweet-Sour Sauce

1 can (13½ oz.) PINEAPPLE CHUNKS
2 tablespoons CORNSTARCH
½ cup VINEGAR
½ cup BROWN SUGAR
2 tablespoons SOY SAUCE
2 tablespoons LEMON JUICE
1 cup GREEN PEPPER (chopped)

Drain pineapple chunks; reserve pineapple. Measure pineapple syrup and add water to make one cup liquid. Blend liquid and cornstarch until smooth.

Stir in next four ingredients. Cook until thickened and clear. Add pineapple chunks and green pepper. Cover and simmer over low heat 15 minutes.

Fresh Orange Glaze for Ham

Grated ORANGE PEEL
  (from 2 large oranges)
½ cup fresh ORANGE JUICE
1 cup BROWN SUGAR (firmly packed)
2 teaspoons DRY MUSTARD
2 tablespoons PREPARED MUSTARD

In small pan, combine all ingredients and boil hard for five minutes, stirring constantly. Set aside and cool to room temperature.

During the final 45 minutes of baking time (before the ham is done), brush or spoon the glaze over ham from time to time.

Thanksgiving Orange Stuffing

6 cups toasted
  BREAD CUBES
½ cup ONION (chopped)
½ cup CELERY (chopped)
1½ cups diced fresh
  ORANGES
1½ teaspoons grated
  ORANGE PEEL

1½ teaspoons THYME
1 CHICKEN BOUILLON
  CUBE with ½ cup
  WATER
      or
½ cup CHICKEN BROTH
SALT and PEPPER

Combine all ingredients. Put mixture into body cavities and close body openings. Roast with turkey, as usual. This stuffing is plentiful for a 12-14 pound turkey, and also adequate for a 14-16 pounder.

Golden Grill Barbecue Sauce

¼ cup SUGAR
2 tablespoons CORN STARCH
½ teaspoon ALLSPICE
½ teaspoon ground CLOVES
1 cup fresh ORANGE JUICE
2 tablespoons VINEGAR
4 tablespoons BUTTER (or margarine)

Combine sugar, corn starch, allspice and cloves in a small saucepan. Slowly stir in orange juice and vinegar. Over medium heat, stir constantly until sauce thickens. Boil three minutes. Stir in butter.

116

Lemon Barbecue Sauce

1/3 cup fresh LEMON JUICE
¼ cup SALAD OIL
3 tablespoons
    WORCESTERSHIRE SAUCE
1 tablespoon ONION POWDER
1½ teaspoon SALT
½ teaspoon GARLIC SALT
Dash of TABASCO

Combine all ingredients in covered jar. Shake well.

Cowpoke Barbecue Sauce

¼ cup BROWN SUGAR
¼ cup SALAD OIL
2 teaspoons SALT
1 teaspoon
    GARLIC POWDER
1 cup VINEGAR

¾ cup fresh LEMON JUICE
2 cups WATER
1 (5-oz.) bottle
    WORCESTERSHIRE
    SAUCE
Dash of TABASCO

Combine all ingredients in saucepan. Bring quickly to boiling point. Reduce heat and simmer for ten minutes. Cool. Pour into one quart container and keep in refrigerator. (Will keep refrigerated for several weeks.)

Cranberry-Orange Relish

4 cups fresh CRANBERRIES
    (uncooked)
2 fresh ORANGES
1½ cups SUGAR

Clean cranberries. Peel oranges, remove any seeds and cut into quarters. Put cranberries and orange pieces thru a food chopper. Add sugar. Mix well and chill in refrigerator. (Makes one quart)

Mince-Spiced Lemon Sauce

1 cup ONION (chopped)
4 tablespoons BUTTER
1 1/3 cups MINCE MEAT
¼ cup fresh LEMON JUICE
¼ cup WATER

Saute onion in butter until golden brown. Stir in mince meat, lemon juice and water. Cook over medium heat just until mixture begins to boil.

117

Hollandaise Sauce

½ cup BUTTER
2 EGG YOLKS
1 tablespoon LEMON JUICE
¼ teaspoon SALT
Dash CAYENNE

Divide butter into three parts. In top of double boiler combine one part butter with egg yolks and lemon juice. Heat over hot water, stirring constantly until butter starts to melt. Add second piece of butter, stirring constantly. As mixture thickens, add third piece of butter. Season with salt and cayenne and serve at once. (For a thinner sauce, add 1/3 cup boiling water to mixture and cook for one minute.)

Mock Hollandaise Sauce

1 cup THICK WHITE SAUCE
2 EGG YOLKS (slightly beaten)
2 tablespoons LEMON JUICE

Prepare white sauce. Add a little hot white sauce to beaten egg yolks and stir. Then pour egg mixture into remaining white sauce. Cook one minute over low heat. Stir in lemon juice and serve immediately over heated vegetables.

Thick White Sauce

3 tablespoons BUTTER (or other fat)
3 tablespoons FLOUR
¼ teaspoon SALT
1 cup MILK

Melt butter (or fat) in heavy saucepan. Blend in flour slowly until smooth. Add salt. Add milk slowly, stirring rapidly to prevent lumping. Bring mixture to a boil, stirring constantly. Reduce heat and cook one minute, stirring constantly. Remove from heat and use for Mock Hollandaise Sauce.

★ ★ ★

Tenderize meats by adding a teaspoon of lemon juice to water in which meat is boiled.

★ ★ ★

To preserve the whiteness of fish, add one tablespoon lemon juice and one-half teaspoon salt to a quart of water when boiling fish.

Freezing Citrus Juices

When tree-fresh citrus is out of season, it is a nice feeling to know you can still enjoy fresh juice. The following is suggested for your home freezer:

Wash fresh citrus, cut in half and juice. Strain the juice through a colander. Pour the juice into freezing containers. (Dry, clean milk cartons are excellent for this purpose.) When pouring juice into containers, leave head space (from 1 inch to 2 inches in each container), as the juice will expand when freezing.

To each quart of juice, add 1/8 teaspoon ascorbic acid. This can be purchased at drugstores. (You may omit the ascorbic acid if you plan to use the juice within six months.) Stir the juice and ascorbic acid until dissolved. Then add two tablespoons of sugar to each quart of juice. Freeze immediately.

Juice can be frozen without any additions of ascorbic acid or sugar, but the pulp has a tendency to float when thawed. The addition of sugar will suspend the pulp when thawed. Ascorbic acid serves as a preservative and flavor enhancer.

If you do not enjoy juicing a large amount of fresh fruit for freezing purposes, purchase FRESH orange juice. Many fruit stands sell fresh orange juice (a word of caution though, be sure to inquire whether the juice is truly fresh and has no additives.) Follow directions for freezing given above.

Grapefruit and tangerine juices can be frozen using the procedure already outlined. Navel oranges are least satisfactory for freezing, as the juice is too heavy and separates too easily. Valencias and other sweet oranges are excellent for juicing purposes.

Freezing Citrus Segments

Select firm, heavy fruit. Wash and peel. Divide into sections, or slice oranges if desired. Remove all membranes and seeds. Pack fruit into freezing containers. (Milk cartons may be used for this purpose.) Cover with syrup, leaving about an inch of head space for expansion. Seal containers and freeze.

Syrup for Freezing Citrus

(This recipe makes approximately 5 cups of a 40% sugar syrup.)

3 cups **SUGAR**
4 Cups **WATER** or **CITRUS JUICE** (chilled)
1/2 teaspoon **ASCORBIC ACID**

Dissolve sugar in cold water or juice. Add the ascorbic acid. (Use a mixture of three cups water to one cup juice for a richer syrup.) Stir to dissolve the sugar. Do not heat.

Another syrup can be made by reducing the amount of sugar to 2 cups and adding 1 cup of light corn syrup. Or, substitute 3/4 cup honey for 1 cup sugar.

Frozen Lemon and Lime Juice

Wash fresh lemons, cut in half and juice. Strain the juice and pour into miniature ice cube trays. Freeze. Remove cubes from tray and place in a plastic bag. Store in freezer and use as needed.

Lemon juice can be frozen in large containers, too. However, the miniature ice cube size is more convenient. When a small amount of juice is called for in a recipe—or, if you wish to use lemon juice in a glass of iced tea—just drop a small cube into the glass and stir. If a small glass of lemonade is called for, drop several of these small cubes into a glass, add water and sugar to taste. Really quick and convenient!

Lime juice can be frozen in the same manner as lemons.

Freezing Whole Oranges

Oranges can be frozen whole, but careful attention is required during thawing. The fruit must not be allowed to thaw completely.

Wash the fruit and dry completely. Place whole fruit in a box or container large enough to hold about 20 to 40 pounds. Put in deep freeze.

Frozen oranges can be used in the following ways:

1) To juice frozen oranges, remove from freezer. Thaw until the fruit can be sliced in half. The center of the fruit should be icy and firm— but not hard—or until an orange juice reamer can grip the pulp without force. Squeeze as fresh fruit.

2) Children go for frozen oranges. Take fruit from freezer and thaw just until a hole a little larger than a soda straw can be cut from the peel. Massage and squeeze orange with hands to soften. Insert soda straw into hole and give to children. As they hold the orange, it will thaw further and provide a cool and healthy refreshment.

3) Adults can enjoy frozen oranges, too! Cut a small cap off the stem end of the fruit. With a pick, poke the fruit until slightly mushy. Add a jigger of your favorite alcoholic beverage and work into pulp. Place fruit in a serving cup. Insert straw and serve at once.

Do not allow fruit to thaw completely! The peel breaks down very rapidly and becomes mushy. However, when used in the semi-frozen state, oranges are wonderfully delicious!

Oranges

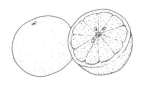

3 to 4 medium = 1 (8-oz.) cup juice

2 medium size = 1 (8-oz.) cup bite size pieces

1 medium size = 4 teaspoons grated peel

1 orange = 10 to 11 sections

Grapefruit

1 medium size = 2/3 cup juice

1 medium size = 1 1/2 cups bite-size pieces

1 medium size = 5 tablespoons grated peel

Lemons

5 to 6 medium size = 1 (8-oz.) cup juice

1 medium size = 3 teaspoons grated peel

Tangerines

5 to 6 medium size = 1 (8-oz.) cup juice

1 medium size = 2 1/2 to 3 teaspoons grated peel

1 peck of citrus = 10 to 15 lbs. of citrus

1/2 bushel of citrus = 24 lbs. of citrus

1 bushel = 50 lbs. of citrus

1 standard size field box = 52 lbs. of citrus

1 standard shipping box = 40 lbs. of citrus

The above approximate equivalents will help you plan the amounts of fruit needed for these recipes. The bottom table has been included to help you estimate the weights of standard containers when buying in bulk from a grower.

INDEX

A

Ambrosia, Jellied, 48
--Southern, 47
--Sunshine, 47
Appetizers, 9-12
Apple Grapefruit Butter, 107
Apricot Grapefruit Ice, 48

B

Baked Grapefruit Alaska, 53
Banana Orange Bread, 79
Barbecue Sauces, 111, 116-117
Bavarian Cream, 50, 51
Beets, Harvard, 41
Beverages, 65-73
--Breakfast Bracer, 65
--Breakfast Drink, 65
--Cafe Brulot, 65
--Champagne Punch, 68
--Citrus, 72
--Citrus Cocktail, 68
--Citrus Cooler, 71
--Citrus Punch, 71
--Desert Quencher, 72
--Fresh Lemonade, 66
--Holiday Punch, 70
--Honey Punch, 67
--Hot Buttered Lemonade, 66
--Hot Lemonade Punch, 67
--Hot Spiced Punch, 69
--Icy Orange Shrub, 71
--Lemonade, 66
--Lemonade Base, 70
--New Year Punch, 68
--Orange Carrot Drink, 73
--Orange Drink, 73
--Orange Shake, 73
--Party Punch, 70
--Pick-a-Flavor Soda, 72
--Pick-a-Flavor Syrup, 72
--Sangria Punch, 69
--Spiced Tea, 67
--Spicy Lemonade, 66
--Sunset Punch, 69
--Sunshine Shake, 65
--Verde Punch, 69
Biscuits, Orange, 93
Breads, 74-81
--Banana Orange, 79
--Lemon Chocolate, 81
--Lemon Loaf, 80
--Lemon Nut, 81

--Nutty Orange, 75
--Orange, 77
--Orange Apricot, 76
--Orange Coconut, 76
--Orange Crackling, 79
--Orange Date Nut, 78
--Orange Nut, 74
--Sunny Morning, 74
--Tangy Orange, 75
Breakfast Bracer, 65
Breakfast Drink, 73
Broccoli, 42, 43
Busy Bee Cookies, 86
Butter, Apple-Grapefruit, 107
--Lemon, 114
--Lime, 25

C

Cafe Brulot, 65
Cakes, 82-93
--Golden Orange, 83
--Orange Carrot, 83
--Orange Date, 84
--Orange Nut, 84
--Orange-Orange, 91
--Orange Peanut Butter, 82
--Orange Ring, 88
--Sunny Orange, 82
--Tangerine Cheesecake, 92
--Twelfth Night, 85
--Velvet Orange, 85
Calamondin Marmalade, 106
Candied Orange Slices, 48
Candied Peel, Citrus, 58
--Orange, 57
--Grapefruit, 57
Carrots (Orange Glazed), 40
Cheesecake, 92
Chicken, Fiji Orange, 29
Chicken Lemon Soup, 12
--Lemony Wings, 31
--Orange Barbecued, 29
--Orange Fried, 30
--Spiced, 28
Citron (History), 8
Citrus Cooler, 71
--Cup, 61
--Dressing, Cooked, 19
--Dressing, Low Calorie, 13
--Fruit Cocktail, 11
--Fruit Dressing, 22
--Fruit Soup, 11
--Gels, 56
--Glazed Lamb Roast, 37

P - R

SALSA LOVERS COOK BOOK

More than 180 taste-tempting recipes for salsas that will make every meal a special event! Salsas for salads, appetizers, main dishes, and, even, desserts! Put some salsa in your life! By Susan K. Bollin.

5 1/2 x 8 1/2—128 pages . . . $5.95

CHILI-LOVERS' COOK BOOK

Chili cookoff prize-winning recipes and regional favorites! The best of chili cookery, from mild to fiery, with and without beans. Plus a variety of taste-tempting foods made with chile peppers. 150,000 copies in print! By Al and Mildred Fischer.

5 1/2 x 8 1/2—128 pages . . . $5.95

PECAN LOVERS COOK BOOK

Indulge your pecan passion for pralines, maca-roons, ice cream, bread pudding, rolls, muffins, cakes and cookies, main dishes and a wide variety of tanta-lizing pecan pies. By Mark Blazek.

5 1/2 x 8 1/2 — 120 Pages . . . $6.95

PUMPKIN LOVERS COOK BOOK

It's pumpkin time again! More than 175 recipes for soups, breads, muffins, pies, cakes, cheesecakes, cook-ies, ice cream, and more! Includes pumpkin trivia!

5 1/2 x 8 1/2—128 Pages . . . $6.95

APPLE LOVERS COOK BOOK

Celebrating America's favorite—the apple! 150 reci-pes for main and side dishes, appetizers, salads, breads, muffins, cakes, pies, desserts, beverages, and preserves, all kitchen-tested by Shirley Munson and Jo Nelson.

5 1/2 x 8 1/2 — 120 Pages . . . $6.95

ORDER BLANK

GOLDEN WEST PUBLISHERS

☼ 4113 N. Longview Ave. • Phoenix, AZ 85014

602-265-4392 • **1-800-658-5830** • FAX 602-279-6901

Qty	Title	Price	Amount
	Apple Lovers Cook Book	**6.95**	
	Arizona Cook Book	**5.95**	
	Best Barbecue Recipes	**5.95**	
	California Country Cook Book	**6.95**	
	Chili-Lovers' Cook Book	**5.95**	
	Chip and Dip Cook Book	**5.95**	
	Christmas in Arizona Cook Book	**8.95**	
	Christmas in New Mexico Cook Book	**8.95**	
	Citrus Lovers Cook Book	**6.95**	
	Cowboy Cartoon Cook Book	**5.95**	
	Easy Recipes for Wild Game & Fish	**6.95**	
	Joy of Muffins	**5.95**	
	Quick-n-Easy Mexican Recipes	**5.95**	
	Mexican Desserts & Drinks	**6.95**	
	Mexican Family Favorites Cook Book	**6.95**	
	Pecan Lovers Cook Book	**6.95**	
	Pumpkin Lovers Cook Book	**6.95**	
	Salsa Lovers Cook Book	**5.95**	
	Texas Cook Book	**5.95**	
	Wholly Frijoles! The Whole Bean Cook Book	**6.95**	
Shipping & Handling Add ➠	U.S. & Canada	$2.00	
	Other countries	$5.00	

☐ My Check or Money Order Enclosed $

☐ MasterCard   ☐ VISA   ($20 credit card minimum)

(Payable in U.S. funds)

Acct. No.   Exp. Date

Signature

Name   Telephone

Address

City/State/Zip

2/96   **Call for FREE catalog**   Citrus Lovers

This order blank may be photo-copied.